Ron Blue is not only a very dedicated and successful CPA and financial planner but also a man with a large (and active) burden to help change the world for the glory of God. I strongly encourage every pastor and concerned layman to read Ron's excellent book *Master Your Money*.

Bill Bright, President
Campus Crusade for Christ

Ron Blue has done an outstanding job of helping us to see our finances from God's perspective. This book should be read by every Christian who handles money—whatever the amount. Read *Master Your Money* and become really "rich."

Paul H. Johnson
Real Estate Developer

Ron Blue has finally made public his revolutionary insights. Brimming with common and uncommon sense, *Master Your Money* reveals practical principles regarding our "treasures," which we can use today and enjoy forever.

Bruce H. Wilkinson, President
Walk Thru the Bible Ministries

Many folks and organizations are what they are today because of the counsel provided by Ron Blue and his organization. Now his book will help sincere Christians better understand their responsibilities as stewards of what God has entrusted to them.

Ted DeMoss, President
Christian Businessmen's
Committee

MASTER YOUR MONEY

Master Your Money

A Step-by-step Plan for Financial Freedom

Ron Blue

THOMAS NELSON PUBLISHERS
Nashville • Camden • New York

Published in Nashville, Tennessee, by Thomas Nelson, Inc., and distributed in Canada by Lawson Falle, Ltd., Cambridge, Ontario.

Printed in the United States of America.

Unless otherwise noted, all Scripture quotations are from THE NEW KING JAMES VERSION. Copyright © 1979, 1980, 1982, Thomas Nelson, Inc., Publishers.

Scripture quotations noted NIV are from The Holy Bible: New International Version. Copyright © 1973, 1978 International Bible Society. Used by permission of Zondervan Bible Publishers.

Holmes and Rahe chart on page 66 reprinted by permission from *Journal of Psychosomatic Research*, T. H. Holmes and R. H. Rahe, "The Social Readjustment Rating Scale," v. 11, 1967, Pergamon Press, Ltd.

Library of Congress Cataloging-in-publication Data

Blue, Ron, 1942–
  Master your money.

  Bibliography: p. 235
  1. Finance, Personal. I. Title.
HG179.B565 1986   332.024   86–18138
ISBN 0-8407-5541-4

CONTENTS

ACKNOWLEDGMENTS

THERE ARE MANY to whom I owe a deep debt of gratitude, beginning with my parents, Don and Emma Blue, who have been a source of encouragement throughout my life.

My wife, Judy, and five children, Cynthia, Denise, Karen, Tim, and Michael, in spite of suffering through the writing of this book, have given me constant encouragement and joy! It is because of my wife that I came to know Jesus Christ as my personal Savior, and her unswerving godly walk the last fourteen years has been a source of spiritual encouragement and challenge.

Ralph and Anne Walls of Indianapolis, Indiana, have been our spiritual parents, friends, partners, clients, and counselors throughout the last fourteen years.

Howie and Jeanne Hendricks of Dallas, Texas, were the ones who initially challenged me into my current business. They are faithful and trusted advisors.

For years, two special friends, Bruce Wilkinson of Atlanta, Georgia, and Dr. Bert Harned of Mesa, Arizona, have encouraged me to write this book.

Bruce Cook of Atlanta and Steve Douglass of San Bernardino, California, with whom I worked on the "I Found It" campaign, provided much of the material on goal setting and faith planning found throughout the book.

Larry Burkett of Dahlonega, Georgia, the nationally recognized authority on biblical principles of finance, has been a source of information and faithful support throughout the last nine years. He is a man I deeply respect and admire.

George and Marjean Fooshee of Wichita, Kansas, and Howard Dayton of Orlando, Florida, each wrote books on financial planning long before I did and had a major impact on my thinking as a financial planner.

Chuck and Cynthia Swindoll of Fullerton, California, have graciously given of their time and experience in helping me work through many of the difficult issues that come in tackling a project such as this. God has blessed me with having them as an example and in watching their "walk" match their "talk."

My partners and staff have been very patient with me during this process, but especially Mina Breeden, my secretary of nine years, and Regina Kreiner who have faithfully typed and edited this book, often working on short notice and with many other demands upon their time. I am indeed grateful for their work.

Etta Wilson, my editor at Thomas Nelson, has been very kind and gentle to me during the editing process, and I appreciate her very much.

Lastly, but most importantly, my Lord and Savior, Jesus Christ, has again proved Himself to be faithful, and apart from Him I would have nothing to say.

FOREWORD

I AM NO authority when it comes to money matters.

Because this is true I have needed to seek help from those who are. While I may not know much about the subject of finances, I am a fairly good judge of character traits like integrity, authenticity, spiritual sensitivity, biblical awareness, and genuine humility. When someone possesses these qualities in addition to professional competence in the sometimes complicated world of finance, I sit up and take notice . . . which explains why Ron Blue and I have cultivated such a close friendship.

For quite some time I have admired his convictions, sought his counsel, listened to his advice, and put his principles to the test. I have yet to regret one moment of that process. He is a rare find in this day of rapid-fire, hit-from-the-hip high-rollers who talk the language but fail to pattern their lives according to scriptural standards. This is what I appreciate most about Ron—he models his message. Quietly, graciously, thoroughly, the man represents what he presents. Because he keeps it so simple, even I can understand it! And that, my friend, is a minor miracle.

Over a year ago I suggested to Ron that he dedicate himself to publishing his material. It seemed a shame that such resourceful and helpful information be available to so few. I am delighted he took up the challenge and disciplined himself to putting his valuable knowledge and techniques into print.

His book addresses numerous subjects that are of interest to all of us: developing a biblical philosophy of personal finances, taking advantage of inflationary times, getting (and staying) out of debt, establishing financial goals, achieving financial independence, overcoming consumptive spending, exposing many tax-planning myths, and cultivating the joy of generous giving as God designed for His people—to name only a few. I especially appreciate the practical, easy-to-understand approach Ron has maintained through these pages. His diagrams, worksheets, and illustrations, and even a glossary of terms take away all the mumbo jumbo, so that readers who lack sophisticated expertise in the field of economics have no trouble grasping and implementing his insights.

Having watched large audiences respond so enthusiastically to Ron's seminars and having experienced the benefits of his capable instruction personally, I am pleased to place my endorsement on this book. I recommend it to you without the slightest reservation.

If your desire is to "master your money" so that greater control and contentment begin to characterize your life, you have selected the right book. It won't take you long to realize that my friend has the right perspective on money, because he is in touch with the right Master.

Chuck Swindoll
Pastor, Radio Bible Teacher, Author

1

Will I Ever Have Enough?

AT THE AGE of 24, I had every ingredient needed for success—an MBA degree, my CPA certificate, a well-paying job with the world's largest CPA firm in their New York City office, a driving ambition to be a success, and a supportive and very intelligent wife.

For the next eight years, I proved to myself that anyone could succeed by really putting everything into it. By the time I was 32 years old, I had achieved every financial and success goal I had set:

- I had moved rapidly up the corporate ladder.
- I had founded the fastest growing CPA firm in Indiana and today it has become one of the larger firms in Indiana.
- I, along with others, owned two small banks in Indiana.
- I had a lovely wife and three young daughters.
- I had all of the trappings of success, a new home, new cars, country club memberships, and the like.

I had also just committed my life to Jesus Christ and had no needs that I was aware of.

It was during the early seventies, and for the first time in the nation's history, Americans began experiencing "tremendous" inflation rates of 4% and 5%. The prime rate hit an unbelievable high of 10% and then even went to 12%. The dollar was taken off the gold standard, and for the first time in recent history, the United States began running a trade deficit.

In the midst of personal affluence, I began to experience the fear that comes from wondering, *Will I ever have enough?* Or, *If I do have enough now, will it be enough when I retire?* And, *By the way, how much is enough?* I believe that everyone, rich and poor, asks themselves these underlying questions more frequently than they would like to admit. These questions are constantly in our subconscious, and therefore we all deal with them somehow—on one hand by hoarding our resources, on the other hand by living out the philosophy of "get all the *gusto* you can—you only go around once."

The Christian, *additionally,* is confronted with the question, What is the appropriate Christian lifestyle? This book, by the grace of God, will attempt to answer each of these questions by providing a framework of financial planning that is both biblical and relevant in our unique society.

Through the midseventies, I dealt with these questions, both personally and as an advisor to a largely wealthy secular clientele. In 1977 my wife and I experienced God's call to leave the businesses I was involved in and join a new ministry in Atlanta, Georgia. For two years, as our family grew to five children, I helped to develop seminar materials in the areas of decision making, time management, faith planning and problem solving. Also during the late seventies, I traveled to Africa 11 times, assisting a large Christian organization to apply the principles that we were developing.

I observed during all of this that the same financial questions that my former clients and I had been asking were being asked by others as well: missionaries, affluent Africans, poor Africans, full-time Christian workers, successful American executives, pastors and friends:

- Will I ever have enough?
- Will it continue to be enough?
- How much is enough?

The questions transcended cultures as well as classes.

In 1979, at the encouragement of Dr. Howard Hendricks, I founded an organization called Christian Financial Management, which has as its objective to remove the fear and frustration that Christians experience when they deal with money. The need for this type of counsel and advice is, I believe, *pervasive.* Christian teaching and application go from the extreme of sharing personal income in communal living to the "name it, claim it" approach. Both are an attempt to *reach* God in the way we handle our money, when all the time He is reaching out to us with His wisdom, counsel, and principles.

This book outlines the journey that my wife and I are on to "be filled with the knowledge of His will in all wisdom and spiritual understanding" (Col. 1:9) as it specifically relates to personal money management for the Christian in the context of a very uncertain economic future.

THE RICH AND THE POOR

According to the Social Security Administration, only 2% of Americans reach age 65 financially independent; 30% are dependent on charity; 23% must continue to work; and 45% are dependent on relatives. Additionally, according to Social Security records, 85 out of 100 Americans have less than $250, when they reach age 65. According to Devney's Economic Tables, fewer men are worth $100 at age 68 than they were at age 18—after 50 years of hard work. In other words, they have worked for 50 years and have not been able to save at least $2.00 each year. Why?

Other staggering statistics were reported in *The Atlanta Journal*—11 out of 12 women will become widows, and the average age of widows in the United States is 52. This, of course, means that most women will have to become money managers someday. Coupled with the facts in the previous paragraph, most will do so with inadequate resources.

The obvious frightening conclusion is that in the world's most affluent society in all of history very, very few individuals ever achieve a position of being able to live off the resources they have accumulated. The vast majority are dependent on government, relatives, charity, or they must continue to work in order to have enough income to meet their needs. And yet there are exceptions, and I have had the privilege of meeting and working with many people who are better prepared for their future.

One of the dramatic exceptions is that of a retired pastor who never earned more than $8,000 in one year. I met this humble man because he wanted to know if he had enough financial resources to live out the rest of his life. At the time of his question, he was 80 years old; he had been retired for 20 years; and his wife had just been put under full-time nursing care. His question, therefore, was a justifiable one!

As I generally do, I began to ask some questions myself before giving advice. First, I asked him if he had any debts. His response was, "No," and he went on to say he had never borrowed any money. I said, "Why not?" He said because if he borrowed money, he would have to pay it back someday, and he couldn't afford to pay off debt, feed his family, and tithe.

My second question was to ask what resources he presently had. He indicated that in his wife's name, he had approximately $250,000 in cash, money market funds, and certificates of deposit. Additionally, in his name, he had another $350,000 in cash and cash-type investments. Needless to say, I was impressed! Over $600,000 in cash accumulated by a couple who had never earned more than $8,000 per year!

One thing bothered me though. He had not yet mentioned any stock investments, and yet in looking at his tax returns, I noticed a substantial amount of dividend income. He revealed that at retirement he had invested approximately $10,000 in the stock of a new company, and at the present time, the market value of his stock in that company was $1,063,000. WOW! *$1,663,000* of cash and stock and they had never earned more than $8,000 per year!

This couple was unusual, but many of the couples whom my firm works with are headed in the same direction. They practice some very basic biblical principles that work regardless of the economy or economic environment. Incidentally, my advice to this man was not to seek advice from anyone, myself included, as we might "mess him up." I said I would be better off listening to him. This couple had followed four basic economic principles that will work for anyone regardless of the economic uncertainty. We will examine those principles in Chapter 2.

DEBTORS ALL

The 40 years following World War II have seen an incredible growth in our affluence as a nation. No people, ever, have possessed the material resources that we do. We are truly a blessed people, and yet there are some significant cracks in our economic structure.

Our national debt (the amount of money owed by our government) recently went over two trillion dollars, or approximately $10,000 for every man, woman, and child in our country. If we wanted to pay off this debt, we would first of all have to stop going into debt; and then if we started a repayment plan of one million dollars per day, it would still take over 2,000 years to pay back the debt. We have mortgaged not only our children's future, but obligated countless future generations. Someone must pay this debt through a literal repayment (future taxes), a deceitful repayment (future inflation) or cancellation (political upheaval). There are no other alternatives. The debt will not merely disappear.

I could go on and on about how serious our economic problems are. For example, what happens to our banking system if Third World countries refuse to repay their debts to American banks? The fact of the matter is, the problems are serious, and there is absolutely nothing that you or I, as individuals, can do to solve them.

More than 200 years ago, while the original 13 colonies were still part of Great Britain, Professor Alexander Tyler wrote of the Athenian republic, which had fallen 2,000 years earlier:

> A democracy cannot exist as a permanent form of government. It can only exist until the voters discover that they can vote themselves a largesse from the [public] treasury. From that moment on, the majority will always vote for the candidates promising the most benefits from the public treasury, with the result that a democracy always collapses over loose fiscal policy and is always followed by a dictatorship.
>
> The average age of the world's greatest civilizations has been 200 years. These nations have progressed through this sequence: From BONDAGE to SPIRITUAL FAITH; from SPIRITUAL FAITH to GREAT COURAGE; from GREAT COURAGE to ABUNDANCE; from ABUNDANCE to SELFISHNESS; from SELFISHNESS to COMPLACENCY; from COMPLACENCY to APATHY; from APATHY to DEPENDENCY; from DEPENDENCY back again into BONDAGE.

There is no question that the United States is at least at the abundance level in the sequence outlined by Professor Tyler. In my opinion we are leaving the selfishness level and approaching complacency.

Before you wring your hands in despair, let me give you a question to ponder. Do you think God is worried? Is He wringing His hands in despair, wondering how it is all going to turn out? Of course not! Inflation, deflation, monetary collapse, and political upheavals are nothing new to Him; and His message is just as relevant today as it was 4,000 years ago.

The context then of personal money management is that God is still in control and under His control there are only four possible economic situations: (1) inflation, (2) deflation, (3) monetary collapse, or (4) political upheaval. There are no other possibilities. Although I am neither an economist nor a prophet and I do not know what is going to happen, I can plan for possible eventualities, and base my planning on basic biblical financial principles. Just a few years ago, almost everyone was projecting increasing double-digit inflation. One of the consequences of that belief was a rapid escalation in raw land prices, especially farm land. However, farm land can be purchased today for one-third to one-half of what it was selling for just three years ago. Almost no one saw the collapse in farm land prices or oil prices, and the consequent devastation to many families, corporations, and even cities (e.g., Houston). The point is, neither inflation nor deflation is a sure thing.

My opinion about what is going to happen is based on the nature of all people to be selfish. A selfish person placed in an environment of almost unlimited opportunity to be selfish (our country, or any shopping mall) will always react with greed. If greed can be funded on an unlimited basis (consumer debt), it will produce inflation. Prices will rise because, with the unlimited opportunity for debt, only the payment is relevant. Inflation, over time, will always produce a monetary collapse because the currency used has become worthless. To put all this in an equation:

Selfishness + productivity = greed
Greed + debt = inflation
Inflation + time = monetary collapse

Do I believe this will really occur? Yes, I do believe it will happen; but God is sovereign and can change the course of our history in any way He wants.

In any case, financial planning *must* take place under the sovereignty of God, recognizing His omnipotence, wisdom, purposes, and plans. Because there are only four economic possibilities, I must plan for all *four* in answering three primary questions:

Will I ever have enough?
Will it continue to be enough?
How much is enough?

I believe that God is more interested in each of us individually than He is in any failure or success of our economic system. I do not believe that the Bible sets forth any one economic system. God is interested in how I glorify Him wherever I live, under capitalism, communism, socialism, or any other system.

God has called each of us to a unique role in an uncertain economy.

2

Four Biblical Principles
of
Money Management

AN ACQUAINTANCE OF mine, William C. Cook, wrote a book called *Success, Motivation and the Scriptures,* in which he defined success as "the continued achievement of God-given goals." I once asked my oldest child how her friends would define success, and she gave me the best worldly definition of success I have ever heard: "To have whatever you want whenever you want it."

One perspective is eternal (long-term) and the other is exceedingly short-term: "I want what I want when I want it." Not only do I want what I want when I want it, but I have a right to it.

Both the Christian and the non-Christian are concerned with success, but in each case success is always relative to goals. The difference is in perspective. One view sees only the here and now, the other sees the unseen. What one's perspective is (or to put it another way, what one believes) will determine attitudes and actions. That is why the Christian, in managing his or her money, is different.

Individually, God has called us to be: salt and light (see Matt. 5:13–16), servants (see Mark 10:45), and stewards (see Matt. 25:14–30).

The idea of being salt and light says that God wants me to be *not* better than, *but* different from. The Christian, therefore, may or may not have more than his neighbor, but that does not distinguish him. What does distinguish the Christian from the world is the absence of any anxiety, which might have come as a result of the loss of something he has managed or even God's denial of something he wants. Why? Because the Christian's treasure is not on earth. The world and its temporal toys do not possess him. He is prayerful, but not the least bit anxious about the tremendous uncertainty facing our national and world economy.

Obviously that attitude is not "normal" but rather "different," and it comes from having an entirely different perspective. The Christian's perspective is eternal, the attitude is one of holding possessions lightly, and the lifestyle is free from worry and anxiety. Truly that is different!

Not only have I been called to be salt and light, but I, and all other Christians, have been called to be a *servant*. "For even the Son of Man did not come to be served, but to serve, and to give His life a ransom for many," says Mark 10:45. Money is one of the most significant resources with which American Christians can serve others. It is not the only resource—time and talents are two others, but it is certainly in greater abundance among American Christians than among non-Americans.

By contrast, the world, one way or another, says that you need to serve yourself: "I want what I want when I want it." God says, "Let them do good, that they be rich in good works, ready to give, willing to share" (1 Tim. 6:18).

Americans are known as generous people. But exactly how generous are we?

- According to the IRS, 1.7% of adjusted gross income is the average charitable deduction taken on Form 1040, whereas the property tax and interest deduction (as indicators of the possessions that the bank and I own) is equal to 18% of adjusted gross income.
- Sam Erickson of the Christian Legal Society once did a personal study of average charitable giving. His conclusion was that all Americans gave, on the average, 25¢ a day or $91 per year, and evangelical Christians gave an average of $1 a day or $365 per year.
- J. Robertson McQuilkin, president of Columbia Bible College, pointed out in a speech that if members of the Southern Baptist denomination alone would give an average of $100 per year to foreign missions, over $1.4 billion per year would be given. They are nowhere near that level now. If they were, the fulfillment of the Great Commission could probably be financed rather easily in this generation by one denomination!

On the other hand, I personally know hundreds of Christians who are serving others by literally giving fortunes away. They have answered the question, Why am I here? One reason you are here is to serve others, and if God has entrusted financial resources to you, you must be used to serve others.

Ultimately, financial planning is the predetermined use of financial resources in order to accomplish certain goals and objectives. The difference in financial planning between the Christian and the non-Christian is the source of the goals and objectives.

John MacArthur, pastor of Grace Community Church, Panorama City, California, in his tape series "Mastery of Materialism," said that "16 out of 38 of Christ's parables deal with money; more is said in the New Testament about money than heaven and hell combined; five times more is said about money than prayer; and while there are 500 plus verses on both prayer and faith, there are over 2,000 verses dealing with money and possessions." Obviously, the Bible has much to say about money management.

THE FOUR BIBLICAL PRINCIPLES OF MONEY MANAGEMENT

Even though the parable of the talents found in Matthew 25:14–30 deals primarily with Christ's return, it has shown me four basic biblical principles of money management that really summarize much of what the Bible has to say regarding money and money management.

1. God Owns It All

Matthew 25:14—"For the kingdom of heaven is like a man traveling to a far country, who called his own servants and delivered his goods to them."

Very few Christians would argue with the principle that God owns it all, and yet if we follow that principle to its natural conclusion, there are three revolutionary implications. First of all, God has the right to whatever He wants whenever He wants it. It is all His, because an owner has *rights,* and I, as a steward, have only *responsibilities.*

When my oldest child reached driving age, she was very eager to use my car and, as her father, I entrusted my car to her. There was never any question that I could take back my car at any time for any reason.

She had only responsibilities while I maintained all the rights. In the same way, every single possession that I have comes from someone else—God. I literally possess much but own nothing.

If you own your own home, take a walk around your property to get a feel for the reality of this principle. Reflect on how long that dirt has been there and how long it will continue to be there; then ask yourself if you really own it or whether you merely possess it. You may have the title to it, but that title reflects your right to possess it temporarily, not forever. Only God literally owns it forever.

If I really believe that God owns it all then when I lose any possession, for whatever reason, my emotions may cry out, but my mind and spirit have not the slightest question as to the right of God to take whatever He wants whenever He wants it. Really believing this also frees me to give generously of God's resources to God's purposes and His people. All that I have belongs to Him.

The second implication of God's owning it all is that not only is my giving decision a spiritual decision, but *every* spending decision is a spiritual decision. There is nothing more spiritual about giving than buying a car, taking a vacation, buying food, paying off debt, paying taxes, and so on. These are all uses of His resources. He owns all that I have.

Think about the freedom of knowing that if God owns it all—and He does—He must have some thoughts about how He wants me to use His property. The Bible reveals many specific guidelines as to how the Owner wants His property used. As a steward, I have a great deal of latitude, but I am still responsible to the Owner. Some day I will give an accounting of how I used His property.

The third implication of the truth that God owns it all is that you can't fake stewardship. Your checkbook reveals all that you really believe about stewardship. A life story could be written from a checkbook. It reflects your goals, priorities, convictions, relationships, and even the use of your time. A person who has been a Christian for even a short while can fake prayer, Bible study, evangelism, going to church, and so on, but he can't fake what his checkbook reveals. Maybe that is why so many of us are so secretive about our personal finances.

2. We Are in a Growth Process

Matthew 25:21—"His lord said to him, 'Well done, good and faithful servant; you were faithful over a few things, I will make you ruler over many things. Enter into the joy of your lord.'"

In reading the Scriptures, it is inescapable not to know that our time on earth is temporary and is to be used by our Lord as a training time. The whole parable emphasizes this. I would observe that God uses money and material possessions in your earthly life during this growth process as *a tool, a test,* and *a testimony.* As Paul said in Philippians 4:11–12:

> Not that I speak in regard to need, for I have learned in whatever state I am, to be content: I know how to be abased, and I know how to abound. Everywhere and in all things I have learned both to be full and to be hungry, both to abound and to suffer need.

Money and material possessions are a very effective tool that God uses to grow you up. Therefore, you need always to ask, God, what do You want me to learn? Not, God, why are You doing this to me? My role as a counselor is to help people discover what God would have them learn, either from the situation of their abundance, or from the situation of their apparent lack of financial resources. God is not trying to frustrate us. He is trying to get our attention and money is a great attention-getter.

Money is not only a tool, but also a test.

> Therefore if you have not been faithful in the unrighteous mammon, who will commit to your trust the true riches? And if you have not been faithful in what is another man's, who will give you what is your own? (Luke 16:11–12).

I don't understand it, but I do know that somehow my eternal position and reward is determined irrevocably by my faithfulness in handling property that has been entrusted to me by God.

We have already looked at the fact that we are called to be salt and light in Matthew 5:13–16. I believe we can say that God can use my use of His resources as a testimony to the world. My attitude as a Christian toward wealth becomes the testimony.

3. The Amount Is Not Important

> Matthew 25:23—"His lord said to him, 'Well done, good and faithful servant; you have been faithful over a few things, I will make you ruler over many things. Enter into the joy of your lord.'"

When you look back to verse 21 and compare it word for word with verse 23, you will see that the same words were spoken to the slave with five talents and the one with two talents. Both were reminded that they had been faithful with a few things and both were promised something in heaven. You can draw the conclusion that the amount you have is unimportant, but how you handle what you have been entrusted with is very important.

There is much controversy today about whether an American Christian is more spiritual on one hand by accumulating much or on the other hand by giving it all away. I believe that both are extremes and not reflective of what God says. He never condemns wealth nor does He commend poverty, or vice versa. The principle found in Scripture is that He owns it all. Therefore, whatever He chooses to entrust you with, hold with an open hand, allowing Him to entrust you with more if He so chooses, or allowing Him to take whatever He wants. It is all His. That is the attitude He wants you to develop, and whatever you have, little or much, your attitude should remain the same.

4. Faith Requires Action

Matthew 25:24–30—"Then he who had received the one talent came and said, 'Lord, I knew you to be a hard man, reaping where you have not sown, and gathering where you have not scattered seed. And I was afraid, and went and hid your talent in the ground. Look, there you have what is yours.' But his lord answered and said to him, 'You wicked and lazy servant, you knew that I reap where I have not sown, and gather where I have not scattered seed. Therefore you ought to have deposited my money with the bankers, and at my coming I would have received back my own with interest. Therefore take the talent from him, and give it to him who has ten talents. For to everyone who has, more will be given, and he will have abundance; but from him who does not have, even what he has will be taken away. And cast the unprofitable servant into the outer darkness. There will be weeping and gnashing of teeth.'"

The wicked slave knew, *but* he did nothing. Many of us know what we ought to do, but we disobey or delay. We have emotional faith and/or intellectual faith, but not volitional faith. We know *but* . . .

We may know deep down what God would have us do, but we are so bombarded with worldly input, which seems to be acceptable, that we are paralyzed. We take no action because of the fear of making a mistake biblically, financially. Or we are frustrated and confused. We do only what we feel good about—and living by our feelings rather than "the truth" (John 14:6) can be very dangerous.

THE PRACTICALITY OF STEWARDSHIP

I will be giving you principles, technical guidance, tools, and techniques for working out *by faith* the unique financial plan that God has for you and your family, so that when you stand before Him you will have confidence and expect Him to say, "Well done, good and faithful servant." Is that hope unrealistic? Not at all. It is God's desire and His intention. He wants it more than you do.

Two points before we begin. First, a working definition of stewardship:

> *Stewardship is the use of God-given resources for the accomplishment of God-given goals.*

This definition is active, not theoretical. It says "use of." Remember that faith requires action. The definition also acknowledges God's ownership over my possessions and His direction of my use of these resources.

Second, on page 24 I would like for you to list anything that you now possess, about which until now you would have said, "This is mine." Then return the ownership of it to its rightful Owner by a simple prayer of commitment, sign the deed, and date it.

You now own nothing and are prepared to be a steward.

Chart 2–A

DEED

On this date I/we acknowledge God's ownership and my/our stewardship responsibility of the following:

ITEM	AMOUNT
_____	_____
_____	_____
_____	_____
_____	_____
_____	_____
_____	_____
_____	_____
_____	_____
_____	_____
_____	_____
_____	_____
_____	_____
_____	_____
_____	_____
_____	_____

Date _____   _____
                               Signature

                               _____
                               Signature

3

A Financial Planning Overview

EACH YEAR FOR Christmas I give my children two sheets of paper as a gift. On them I list several things I can do with them during the next year. Some of the options are: going out for breakfast or lunch, going to a professional baseball, basketball, or football game, or going with me on one of my speaking trips. My objective is to let them pick how they would really like to spend time with me.

It's been interesting to observe the difficulty they have in choosing which activity they really want. One that seems to be a favorite is "spending four hours with me and having $25 to spend in any way you choose." The first year we began this tradition my third daughter, who was nine years old at the time, picked this option and carefully planned our time together. We were to start at a large shopping mall on a Saturday morning and end with lunch. She was filled with anticipation and excitement when the day arrived.

Picture in your mind a nine-year-old child with $25 in her hand, entering a mall with tens of millions of dollars worth of goods available to buy. The dilemma she faced is exactly the same dilemma that you and I face—there is *never* enough money to do or buy everything that you want. There are always more ways to spend money than there is money available. You may respond as she did.

After shopping for just a little while, we went in a store with overpriced notions, such as crazy pens, note paper, and so on, and she selected several items—despite my caution that tomorrow they would not be nearly as attractive. I said to her, "Karen, remember that good decision making requires a long-term perspective." She assured me that she would use and love these items "forever and forever." When the bill was totaled, she had spent her $25 and we still had three hours left and lunch to buy. We ended up going home early so that she could play with her purchases.

The very next day everything she had purchased was either used up, broken, or uninteresting. I will never forget her confessing to me that she had, in effect, responded to the emotion of the moment and, in retrospect, made a poor choice. The problem was that her money and time were both irretrievably lost.

What was not lost, however, was the experience and what it taught her. She frequently says to me now when I am getting ready to buy something, "Daddy, don't forget that the longer term your perspective, the better your decision is likely to be." Sometimes I wish that I hadn't taught her that!

This story illustrates four truths:

1. All of us have limited resources.
2. Consequently, there are more alternative uses of money available than money available.
3. Today's decisions determine destiny. (A dollar spent is gone forever and can never be used in the future for anything else.)
4. The longer the term of perspective, the better is the decision making.

I can summarize these four points by saying that most of us are responders rather than planners. We respond to friends, advertising, and our emotions rather than plan our spending.

> *Financial planning is allocating limited financial resources among various unlimited alternatives.*

When we know for certain what financial resources we have and have planned to use them to accomplish various goals and objectives, our lives take on the contentment of having made order out of chaos. Our frustration in having to choose among the overwhelming multiplicity of alternatives disappears. We are freed from the pressures of the short-term, self-gratifying society around us. We are free to be different.

The financial planning framework that I am going to help you develop will do several things for you: give you a process of managing money; summarize the almost infinite alternative uses of money into just a manageable few; integrate short-range and long-range planning and clearly demonstrate the trade-offs; give you a sense of order and thereby remove some of the guilt or at least the questions that come in using money.

OBJECTIVES OF FINANCIAL PLANNING

One thing I have been implying all along but have never actually stated is that accumulating financial resources should never be an end in itself. They are accumulated solely for the reason of using them to accomplish some purpose, goal, or objective. For example, you do not take a vacation or buy a car just to spend money, but rather to provide something else such as recreation and transportation. Many people ask me how to spend money and I always make it a practice to ask, "What are you really trying to accomplish?" This question helps to focus the decision on real objectives.

In the short range, there are basically only five spending objectives; and, in the long range, only six. Every spending decision or use of money accomplishes one of these 11 objectives.

Short-range Objectives

Figure 3.1 illustrates that there are *only* five short-term alternative uses for all income coming into a household. It can be

1. given away,
2. spent to support a lifestyle,
3. used for the repayment of debt,
4. used to meet tax obligations,
5. accumulated or saved.

Every spending decision, in the short term, will fit into one of these five categories.

How the money is allocated among the five alternatives is a function of just two factors: the *commitments* I already have and my *priorities*. For example, with my wife and five children, I have certain lifestyle commitments that others do not have. Debt repayment, taxes, and giving are all commitments I must maintain. Certain lifestyle expenses such as utilities, food, insurance, and so on are also commitments. A commitment must always be top priority.

Ultimately, my priorities will dictate the allocation of the balance of the limited resources. Giving and accumulation are usually stated as pri-

Figure 3.1

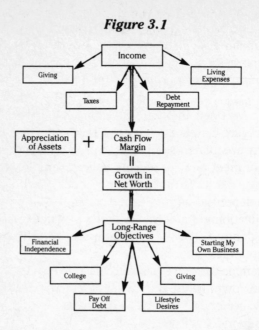

orities, but in reality, they wind up at the bottom of the priority ladder. I have observed that most American Christians have lifestyle as their top priority and second, because of their lifestyle, debt repayment. Taxes would be a third priority because they have no choice; fourth would be accumulation; and finally, giving. The line of reasoning goes this way: *I am already committed to a certain lifestyle and debt schedule, which God surely wouldn't want me to change. I would gladly give up paying my taxes, but I can't. I am giving and would give more if it weren't for the taxes I have to pay and the money I need to set aside for the future because that is good stewardship.*

Of the five short-range uses, three are consumptive in nature and two are productive. Lifestyle expenditures, debt repayment, and taxes are all consumptive in nature; when the money is spent, it is gone forever. Both accumulation and giving are productive uses of money. Money that is put into accumulation is much like planting a crop—later on, much more than what was planted comes up and can be used again for either consumption or production.

The Bible gives us many principles and guidelines about each one of these five areas, but very little in the way of direct commandment. To determine what God would have us do in balancing our priorities requires the discipline of spending time with Him. No one other person, including your financial planner, can tell you how to prioritize your spending. Why? God has not entrusted the resources you possess (but do not own) to someone else; only *you* are accountable for managing the use of God's resources entrusted to you.

Long-term Objectives

In reviewing Figure 3.1, you will note that as we accumulate from our cash flow margin, we grow our net worth, and we grow our net worth for the purpose of meeting one or more of the six long-term objectives:

1. financial independence,
2. college education for children,
3. paying off debt,
4. major lifestyle desires,
5. major charitable giving,
6. owning your own business.

To be financially independent means that the resources accumulated will generate enough income to fund all of the short-range objectives, with the exception of savings. (Savings are no longer needed if enough have accumulated.) When a couple knows what their short-range objectives are, they can easily calculate how large an investment fund is necessary to accumulate what they need in order to be financially independent.

In addition to accumulating for financial independence, couples with children will need to accumulate in order to meet the major expense of college education. That expense can easily be $10,000 or $12,000 per year for each child.

Many couples also have a major long-term goal of being completely out of debt, including the debt on their home. We will discuss the whole issue of debt in Chapter 6, but I believe it is a worthwhile long-term objective to be totally debt free.

The long-range objective of major lifestyle desires is the area that makes each family unique. The objective could be another home, a second home, a new car, a particular vacation, redecorating or remodeling the home, and so on. This type of goal finishes the statement: I want to improve my lifestyle by . . .

One of the first clients whom I worked with at Christian Financial Management was a man who indicated that the most important long-term goal he could think of was to be able to give away at least one million dollars toward the fulfillment of the Great Commission. This was the first time I had ever considered that people may desire to accumulate over the long-term in order to meet a substantial giving goal. This man not only wanted to give the one million dollars before retirement, but he wanted to continue to give at approximately 15% of his total income during the time period that he would be accumulating wealth.

Lastly, you may want to accumulate in order to start your own business, and that is also a legitimate long-range goal.

If you can define and quantify these long-term goals, then you will have answered the question, How much is enough? You know now what your "finish lines" are. It is much like a runner who runs the race until he breaks the tape. Very few runners continue after they have broken the tape. Yet in our financial lives, many of us never stop running because we do not know where the finish line is. We have never quantified where we are headed, and therefore we do not know when we have arrived.

My challenge to you is to determine where you are going, both in the short-term and in the long-term.

INTEGRATED PLANNING

Figure 3.2 puts together the short-term and long-term objectives and outlines a four-step process of financial planning.

Step 1: Summarize your present situation
Step 2: Establish your financial goals
Step 3: Plan to increase your cash flow margin
Step 4: Control your cash flow

I will take you through each step to develop your own unique financial plan in the chapters ahead. If you know where you are, where you are going, and the steps to get there, then you will have made a major step toward being a planner rather than a responder.

As you review the diagram, there are three very important implications. The first is that there are no independent financial decisions. If you make a decision to use financial resources in any one area, by definition, you have chosen not to use those same resources in the other areas. This means that if you choose to set aside money for college education or financial independence, you no longer have that money available to

Figure 3.2

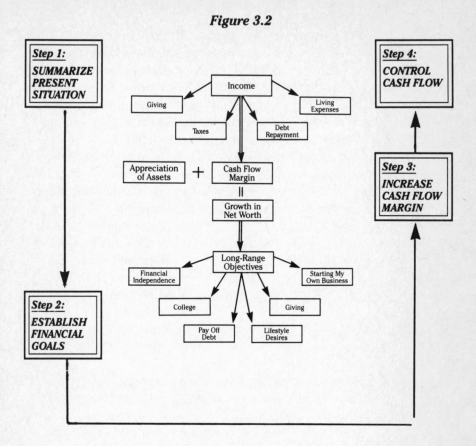

spend on giving, lifestyle desires, debt repayment, and the like. By the same token, if you decide to spend money on lifestyle desires, you no longer have those same resources available for any other short-term or long-term goals.

The second implication, when looking at that diagram, is that the longer the term of your perspective, the better the possibility of your making a good current financial decision. A friend and close confidant once defined financial maturity as "being able to give up today's desires for future benefits." If I choose to give up something today in order to accumulate or save for tomorrow, I have probably made a wise financial decision. The most dramatic example I can think of is the person who chooses a husband or wife. Taking a long-term perspective in that decision makes for a better choice than simply satisfying a short-term need.

The same principle holds true in financial decisions.

The third implication of this diagram is the lifetime nature of financial decisions. I mentioned earlier that three of the uses of money in the short-term are consumptive and two are productive. Any time money is used consumptively, it is gone forever and can never be used for anything in the future. I like to remind those with whom I counsel that *decisions determine destiny*. Once I make a decision either to save or spend, I have determined, to some extent, my destiny.

You, of course, have to accept the truth of this implication—you can't have everything you want when you want it. Success is knowing where you are going in life and knowing how to arrive there.

These goal areas, however, are not what we are really trying to accomplish in life, but rather reflect the real desires of our hearts:

- Security
- Properly trained children
- Peace
- Contentment
- Flexibility
- Comfort
- Personal growth

- Obedience to God
- Transportation
- Rest and relaxation
- Self-worth
- Acceptance
- Sense of belonging
- Other goals . . .

Money, then, is one of the resources you use to accomplish the desires you have. Success is knowing what God would have you to be and do, and how to achieve that, so that when you stand before Him, you will hear Him say, "Well done, good and faithful servant." When money becomes your focus, you are doomed to disappointment, because it is merely a resource and was never intended by the Creator to be anything more than that.

4

Guaranteed Financial Success

RECENTLY I WAS walking from the Sunday morning worship service to my Sunday school class when a teacher stopped me to ask if I could help him with his lesson on stewardship for that morning. The class was to start in just a few minutes, but I agreed to tell him all I could in that brief time. I said a quick prayer asking for wisdom and the thought came to my mind that my basic message is threefold.

> 1. **God owns it all.**
> 2. **Money is never an end in itself, but is merely a resource used to accomplish other goals and obligations.**
> 3. **Spend less than you earn and do it for a long time, and you will be financially successful.**

There is tremendous freedom of mind in knowing and believing that God owns it all, and that money is nothing more than a resource provided by God to allow us to accomplish His purposes on this earth.

Is it wrong then to have a long-term goal of financial independence? I believe not—unless financial independence is defined as having enough to be independent from God. This whole question is really one of "How much is enough?"

How do you achieve one or more of the long-term goals, such as financial independence, college education, improving your lifestyle, getting out of debt, making major contributions, or starting your own business? The answer is simple—spend less than you earn and do it for a

33

long time—or as the Bible says, "He who gathers money little by little makes it grow" (Prov. 13:11 NIV).

For example, if you started supporting yourself at age 20 and for the next 40 years you always spent $1,000 less than you earned and you invested that $1,000 each year in an investment earning at least 12.5% interest, at age 60 you would have an investment fund of $1,000,000. (This computation ignores the tax implications, which we will deal with later.)

Or if you are already at age 40, you can spend $10,000 per year less than you earn, invest it at 12.5% interest, and you can still accumulate the $1,000,000. The 12.5% and $1,000,000 are not magical nor necessarily even desirable, but they do illustrate what has been called the eighth wonder of the world—the "magic of compounding."

The magic of compounding results from the relationship between an interest rate and a time period that can be determined by the "Rule of 72." The Rule of 72 says that any interest rate divided into 72 will always give you the length of time required for an amount to double in value. For example, if you invest $10,000 at an interest rate of 3%, it will take 24 years for the $10,000 to grow to $20,000.

$$3\overline{)72}^{\underline{\ 24\ }\text{years}}$$

If, however, I can earn 6%, the $10,000 will double in only 12 years.

$$6\overline{)72}^{\underline{\ 12\ }\text{years}}$$

To observe the magic of compounding, observe in this table that as you double the interest rate earned, you get a geometric increase in the amount accumulated.

Chart 4–A

		Year 1	Year 12	Year 24	Year 36	Year 48	
	3%	$10,000		$ 20,000		$ 40,000	4 times greater
Double	6%	10,000	$ 20,000	40,000	$ 80,000	160,000	16 times greater
Double	12%	10,000	40,000	160,000	640,000	2,560,000	256 times greater
Double	24%	10,000	160,000	2,560,000	40,960,000	655,360,000	

The magic of compounding results because interest earns interest, which earns interest, which earns interest, which earns interest, *ad infinitum.* In other words, the amount is not nearly so important as the

Chart 4-B
COMPOUNDING
TIME + MONEY + YIELD

DEPOSIT OF A LUMP SUM:
*$10,000 at various interest rates and over various time periods.

END OF YEAR VALUES

	5	10	15	20	25	30	35	40
2%	$11,040	$12,189	$13,458	$14,859	$16,406	$18,113	$19,998	$22,080
4%	12,166	14,802	18,009	21,911	26,658	32,433	39,460	48,010
6%	13,382	17,908	23,969	32,071	42,918	57,434	76,860	102,857
8%	14,693	21,589	31,721	46,609	68,484	100,626	147,853	217,245
10%	16,105	25,937	41,772	67,274	108,347	174,494	281,024	492,592
12%	17,623	31,058	54,735	96,462	170,000	299,599	527,996	930,509
14%	19,254	37,072	71,379	137,434	264,619	509,501	981,001	1,888,835
16%	21,003	44,114	92,655	194,607	408,742	858,498	1,803,140	3,787,211
18%	22,877	52,338	119,737	273,930	626,686	1,433,706	3,279,972	7,503,783
20%	24,883	61,917	154,070	383,375	953,962	2,373,763	5,906,682	14,697,606
22%	27,027	73,046	197,422	533,576	1,442,101	3,897,578	10,534,018	28,470,377
24%	29,316	85,944	251,956	738,641	2,165,419	6,348,199	18,610,540	54,559,126
25%	30,517	93,132	284,217	867,361	2,646,698	8,077,935	24,651,903	75,231,638

Chart 4-C

END OF YEAR VALUES

DEPOSIT OF AN ANNUAL AMOUNT:
*$1,000 per year.

	5	10	15	20	25	30	35	40
5%	$ 5,525	$12,578	$ 21,578	$ 33,065	$ 47,727	$ 66,439	$ 90,320	$ 120,800
8%	5,867	14,487	27,152	45,762	73,106	113,283	172,317	259,056
10%	6,105	15,937	31,772	57,275	98,347	164,494	271,024	442,593
12%	6,353	17,548	37,279	72,052	133,333	241,332	431,663	767,091
16%	6,877	21,321	51,660	115,380	249,214	530,312	1,120,713	2,360,757
20%	7,442	25,959	72,035	186,688	471,981	1,181,882	2,948,341	7,343,858
24%	8,048	31,643	100,815	303,600	898,092	2,640,916	7,750,225	22,728,802

interest rate and the time period. The earlier you start and the more you earn in interest, *the less you need to start with.*

How important is the interest rate? Look at Chart 4–B on page 35. At 25%, $10,000 grows to $75,231,638 in 40 years, but at 24%, it only grows to $54,559,126 in the same length of time, nearly $21,000,000 difference.

When you look at Chart 4–C and compare the deposit of an annual amount with the deposit of a lump sum in Chart 4–B, you immediately see that it takes much more money over a longer time period to achieve the same results. $10,000 invested initially and never added to, but growing at a compounded rate of 24% per year grows to $54,559,126; whereas $1,000 invested per year for 40 years or a total of $40,000 invested (four times as much) only "grows" to $22,728,812.

Compounding always involves four variables—the amount available, the amount needed, the time period and the earnings rate. If I know three of the variables, I can always determine the fourth from one of the charts.

In 10 years my youngest child, who is now in the second grade, will be starting college. I would like to be able to provide $20,000 toward his college education and let him provide the balance in some way— scholarships, savings, or work. I estimate that I can save $1,000 per year toward that goal. The question is, What earnings rate do I have to achieve?

Known Variables:

Amount desired	$20,000
Time period	10 years
Amount provided	$1,000 per year

1. Go to Chart 4–C (deposit of an annual amount).
2. Look down the 10-year column and find the number closest to $20,000 ($21,321).
3. Determine which row you are in—16%.

Solution—Required earnings rate 16%

If 16% cannot be reasonably achieved, then more than $1,000 per year must be invested or the amount accumulated will not reach the goal, and therefore alternative funding sources for college must be sought.

Using the following form, you can go through this same exercise with each of your long-term goals:

Chart 4–D

	Amount Needed	When Needed	Amount Available	Earnings Rate
Financial Independence	$		$	
College Education				
Pay Off Debt				
Major Lifestyle Desires:				
Car				
Home				
Vacation				
Other				
Giving				
Start Own Business				

At the end of this chapter are several examples (see Table 4.1) you can experiment with, but here is the key point: **You do not have to save $1,000,000 to end up with $1,000,000.** The earlier you start, the less you have to save. The later you start, the more you either have to save or earn in interest (and therefore take more risk).

At this point, you are saying to yourself one or more of the following:

- Why didn't I hear this earlier? It's too late for me.
- Yes, but where can I earn 25%?
- $75,000,000 won't be worth much in 40 years because of inflation.
- He has ignored that I must pay taxes on the interest every year; therefore, the compounding won't work as illustrated.
- I don't care about the future, I want to enjoy the money now.

Let me assure you that not only do I understand these questions, but in some cases, I am still dealing with them on a personal level. All of them will be addressed in the balance of this chapter and the next, but first you must not only understand "the magic of compounding" but also the concept of "margin."

THE CONCEPT OF MARGIN

The retired pastor described in Chapter 1 pointed out to me the guaranteed key to financial success when he said that he "never spent more than he earned." He always tithed, paid his taxes, and lived on what was left.

Look again at our financial planning diagram (see Fig. 4.1) and observe that, first of all, the long-term goals will probably require substantial financial resources, and second, that without receiving either an inheritance or striking oil, the only way to reach your long-term goals is to spend less than you earn over time. In other words, you must plan to have a cash flow margin every year. When you do this and let the magic of compounding work for you, you can be assured, if you start early enough, of reaching your long-term goals.

However, like most of us, you probably already have short-term commitments and priorities that may have you spending more than you

Figure 4.1

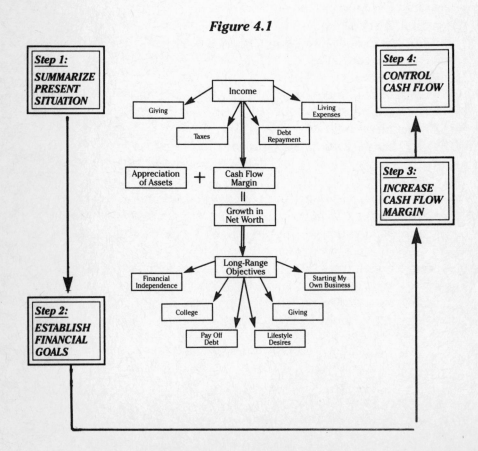

earn or mandate that both spouses must work. Perhaps, and even probably, you are funding your annual negative cash flow margin with increased credit card use or consumer debt. Incidentally, consumer debt is so easy to get because the lenders of money understand very well the magic of compounding. For example, if you pay a lender $1,000 per year for car payments every year during a working life (about 40 years), and the lender in turn lends out your payment to another borrower at 12.5% interest, the lender will have accumulated $1,000,000 from your mere $40,000 of car payments. That works out to be an average annual return of 2,400%!

$1,000,000 − $40,000 = $960,000—the interest earned.

$960,000 ÷ 40 = $24,000—the average interest earned per year.

The point is that you want the magic of compounding working for you instead of against you, and that will happen only if you spend less than you earn. You *must* have a cash flow margin in order to achieve your long-term financial goals.

This is the hard part, because in order to generate enough cash flow margin each year to meet your long-term goals, you have to make the long term a priority over the short term (delayed gratification). So where do you cut? The tithe should not be cut; taxes cannot be cut without either reducing your income or spending cash on some deductible item; debt repayment cannot and should not be cut. The only area left is your lifestyle. However, many lifestyle expenses cannot be cut because of previous commitments such as where you live, how many mouths you have to feed, and so on. The world, in the form of advertisers, friends, neighbors, other Christians and even Christian leaders, would lead you to believe that you are owed or have a right to a lifestyle that may very well be beyond what you can afford.

I believe it is easy to know what lifestyle God has chosen for you by working through the following financial planning diagram:

Chart 4–E

Total income	$_____
Less: tithe	(_____)
Less: taxes (all)	(_____)
Less: debt repayment	(_____)
Less: savings for long-term	(_____)
Balance	$_____

The balance left is the amount available for the funding of a lifestyle. Granted, this may seem simplistic, but God's answers don't have to be difficult. It is also true that you may not achieve the lifestyle level you are seeking immediately, that the tithe is just the beginning of giving, that planning can impact the amount paid in taxes, and that God may choose to increase your income; but to presume any of these things will happen is a violation of a biblical principle. (See James 4:13–17.)

The point is that you must plan to have a cash flow margin if you are going to achieve your long-term goals, and the only truly discretionary place to cut spending, in order to generate this margin, is in the area of lifestyle. However, to do so will be very, very, very difficult because there will be no worldly support and very little Christian support. Frankly, only by the grace of God can it be done, but in Chapter 9, I will share with you all that I know about the ways to reduce living expenses, and in Chapter 6, I will show you how to get out of debt and stay out. (Living expenses and debt are intertwined in American society.)

CONCLUSION

Putting the concept of cash flow margin with the magic of compounding gives these conclusions:

1. *Get rich slowly.* Accumulation of financial resources is not difficult—it merely requires patience and self-discipline; both are fruits of the Spirit. It is not necessary to save $1,000,000 in order to have a $1,000,000. Again, *I am not suggesting that this should even be your goal,* but rather that accumulation for long-term goals is not nearly as difficult as one might think. The Bible says, "He who gathers money little by little makes it grow"; and I would paraphrase that to say, "You can't eat an elephant in one bite, but you can eat an elephant one bite at a time."

2. *There is an opportunity cost to consumption.* A dollar spent today does *not* take a dollar out of the future; it takes *multiple* dollars. Only $2.74 per day spent on nonproductive purchases results in an overspending of $1,000 per year. If that $1,000 per year were instead invested so as to earn 12.5% compounded annually (such as in an IRA), then the $2.74 per day cost me the $1,000,000 that I could have had. The next time you make a spontaneous purchase, ask yourself, What does this really cost me? Likewise, losses on investments or mistakes on major purchases, such as cars, cost far

more than it appears because not only must the loss be made up but also what that loss would have earned in the intervening time must be made up.

3. *Money has time value.* The amount that I have today is worth far more in the future than it is today, assuming that it can earn something each year.

Table 4.1

EXAMPLE 1: Required earnings rate
  Known Variables:

Amount available	$1,000 per year
Amount needed	$100,000
When needed (time period)	20 years

SOLUTION—Earnings rate—16%
  1. Go to Chart 4–C, page 35 (deposit of an annual amount).
  2. Come down the 20-year column to the number closest to $100,000.
  3. Go across to the earnings rate percentage to see what percentage is required.

EXAMPLE 2: Time it will take to accumulate a required amount
  Known Variables:

Amount available	$10,000 now
Amount needed	$50,000
Earnings rate attainable	8%

SOLUTION—Time required—20 years plus
  1. Go to Chart 4–B, page 35 (deposit of a lump sum).
  2. Come down the earnings rate column to 8%.
  3. Go across to find the amount closest to $50,000.
  4. Determine which "years" column you are in.

EXAMPLE 3: Amount that will be accumulated
  Known Variables:

Amount available	$5,000 per year
Earnings rate attainable	12%
Time period I can save and earn	15 years

SOLUTION—Amount that will be accumulated—$186,395
  1. Go to Chart 4–C (deposit of an annual amount).
  2. Come down the 15-year column to the point where it intersects the 12% row and determine the number—$37,279.
  3. Multiply that number $37,279×5 ($5,000 per year is 5×$1,000 per year).

EXAMPLE 4: How much needs to be invested each year
   Known Variables:
       Amount needed $50,000
       Earnings rate attainable   10%
       When needed (time period)   10 years

SOLUTION—Amount required to be invested each year—$2,852
   1. Go to Chart 4–C (deposit of an annual amount).
   2. Find the number at the intersection of the 10-year column and 10% row ($17,530). This is the amount that $1,000 invested each year at a 10% earnings rate will grow to.
   3. Divide $50,000 by $17,530 and multiply the result 2.852×$1,000. In other words, it takes 2.852×$1,000 per year to achieve $50,000 in 10 years at an earnings rate of 10%, since $1,000 per year at 10% for 10 years will only grow to $17,530.

5

CHAPTER

The Myths of Inflation

OVER THE LAST several years I have had the privilege of traveling all over this country and speaking to literally thousands of people. At some point during many of my presentations, I often ask for everyone in the audience who believes that inflation is dead to raise his hand. To date, absolutely no one has ever raised a hand, and yet inflation is relatively low today, especially when compared to the late seventies. As I stated earlier, I am not a prophet. Nevertheless, I believe the very basic nature of man will force inflation on our society, and there is nothing that you and I can do about it except plan for it.

A good description of the effects of inflation is found in Haggai 1:6: "You have sown much, and bring in little; / You eat, but do not have enough; / You drink, but you are not filled with drink; / You clothe

Chart 5–A

INFLATION ILLUSTRATION: FUTURE EQUIVALENTS

YEARS UNTIL RETIREMENT	EXPECTED INFLATION RATE				
	6%	8%	10%	12%	14%
5	1.34	1.47	1.61	1.76	1.92
10	1.79	2.16	2.59	3.11	3.70
15	2.40	3.17	4.18	5.47	7.14
20	3.21	4.66	6.73	9.65	13.74
25	4.29	6.85	10.83	17.00	26.46
30	5.74	10.06	17.45	29.96	50.95
35	7.69	14.79	28.10	52.90	98.10
40	10.29	21.73	45.26	93.05	188.88

yourselves, but no one is warm; / And he who earns wages, / Earns wages to put into a bag with holes."

The problem with inflation is twofold, and both problems cause fear. First of all, inflation destroys the purchasing power of the money already accumulated, and second, it requires that you continually earn more just to stay even with the increasing costs for the goods and services you need to live on. This is true because inflation has a compounding effect that makes the magic of compounding work against us.

For example, you can look at the different inflation assumptions in Chart 5–A on page 43 and determine what income you will need at retirement in order to have the same relative income as you have now. A couple earning $30,000 a year now will have to earn 5.74 times as much or $172,200 a year in 30 years just to have the same relative income if we have an inflation rate of merely 6%. If the inflation rate for those 30 years is 10% rather than 6% (only 4% more), the relative increase will need to be 17.45 times $30,000 or $523,500.

It is no wonder that Dwight Eisenhower identified inflation as one of the major problems facing our nation when he left office in 1960—and the inflation rate then was a mere 1.5%! In fact, high levels of inflation in our country are a very recent phenomenon. Look at Figure 5.1 on page 45.

The problem today is not so much inflation as it is the fear of inflation. One of the results of this fear of the future is that we have become a "now" society. Too many of us adopt the philosophy that it will never be any cheaper than it is now, and besides, we only go around once.

Out of this fear and emphasis on the now have evolved four basic myths regarding inflation. They are: (1) Buy it now, because it will cost more later. (2) You should always borrow to buy (the use of OPM—"other people's money"). (3) You can never accumulate enough. (4) The rate of inflation is standard for everyone.

These myths have just enough truth in them to make them believable, and many people govern their economic lives by them.

In the summer of 1983 a man came into my office and as we were discussing his financial situation, he made a startling statement. "I sure wish we would go back to double-digit inflation," he commented. I was surprised and asked him to explain what he meant. He said that during the early eighties he had been earning 18%, 19%, and 20% on the money he had invested in a money market fund. However, since the inflation rate had been reduced, he was earning substantially less on his

Figure 5.1

INFLATION RATES, 1950–1985

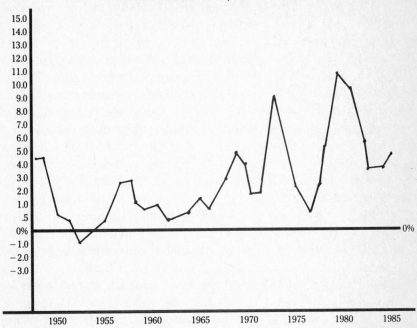

investment. He had never made so much money as when we had double-digit inflation!

His statement was exactly right, and his experience is the experience of history. During times of inflation, the magic of compounding can either work for you or against you, depending on whether you are borrowing money (negative compounding) or lending money as an investor (positive compounding). When I discussed this with a banker friend, he described a study done by some Swiss bankers which showed that over the last 700 years, the average annual rate of interest charged for loans was approximately 3% greater than the average annual inflation rate. So, the real rate of return to the lender was 3%, not the 5%, 10%, 12%, and the like, that they actually charged. If this is true, then everyone lending money (which we do when we put money into any kind of savings fund) should be able to average, over the long run, at least 3% more than the inflation rate. This is extremely important because, if it is true, by being on the lending side of inflation, you will have the magic of compounding working for you, and you will *always beat inflation*. No longer is it something to be feared!

I am not advocating inflation, because in the long run it destroys a currency and undermines the economic and political system. However, if we are destined to have inflation, it should, at the very least, work for us rather than against us.

The chart on the opposite page illustrates that over the last 20 years, investing in short-term money market instruments (i.e., being a lender to a financial institution or business) has consistently been a way to beat inflation. Other investments have done even better than the money market instruments; however, they are riskier, require expertise to select and manage, and in many cases have poor liquidity. The point, again, is that by having a consistent cash flow margin (spending less than you earn), it is possible to have the magic of compounding work for you rather than against you.

The fact that the interest earned will be taxed does make a significant difference in how much can ultimately be accumulated. For example, $2,000 per year invested in something that is either tax exempt or tax deferred, such as an IRA that yields 12% per year, will grow to $144,104 in 20 years and $1,534,182 in 40 years, whereas the same amount invested to yield 8% after tax (a 33% tax rate) will grow to $91,424 in 20 years and only $518,112 in 40 years—over $1,000,000 less, just because of the taxes paid on the earnings each year.

The important point is the "real interest rate," not the stated rate. Historically, the real interest rate has beaten inflation by 3%, but taxes can destroy this spread unless taxes and income are indexed for inflation. This is exactly what happens in countries that experience high inflation rates, and it has already happened in our country.

Understanding the magic of compounding, the concept of margin and the *real* interest rates prepares us to deal with the myths of inflation. We must also remember that God is sovereign and can superintend His will into any personal financial situation or political system.

Myth 1: Buy Now Because It Will Cost More Later

This statement appears to make good financial sense at first reading, but it presupposes that you absolutely will need the item you are buying in the future. The real question then is not what it costs or what it will cost, but rather do you need it? The myth encourages us to delude ourselves into funding our *greeds* rather than our *needs*. Advertisers really

Chart 5–B

Year Ending Dec. 31	Inflation Rate	High Grade Corp. Bonds	Real Rate	4–6 Month Com'l. Paper	Real Rate
1950	5.8	2.6	—3.2	1.7	4.1
1951	5.9	3.1	—2.8	2.3	3.6
1952	0.9	3.0	2.1	2.3	1.4
1953	0.6	3.1	2.5	2.3	1.7
1954	—0.5	2.9	3.4	1.3	1.8
1955	0.4	3.1	2.7	3.0	2.6
1956	2.9	3.4	0.5	3.6	0.7
1957	3.0	3.7	0.7	3.8	0.8
1958	1.8	4.1	2.3	3.3	1.5
1959	1.5	4.6	3.1	4.9	3.4
1960	1.5	4.4	2.9	3.2	1.7
1961	0.7	4.4	3.7	3.2	2.5
1962	1.2	4.2	3.0	3.3	1.1
1963	1.6	4.4	2.8	4.0	2.4
1964	1.2	4.4	3.2	4.2	3.0
1965	1.9	4.7	2.8	4.7	2.8
1966	3.4	5.3	1.9	6.0	2.6
1967	3.0	6.9	3.9	5.6	2.6
1968	4.7	6.5	1.8	6.1	1.4
1969	6.1	7.8	1.7	8.8	2.7
1970	5.5	7.4	1.9	5.7	0.2
1971	3.4	7.1	3.7	6.0	2.6
1972	3.4	7.2	3.8	5.5	2.1
1973	8.8	7.7	—1.1	9.1	0.3
1974	12.2	8.6	—3.6	9.0	3.2
1975	7.0	8.6	1.6	6.0	1.0
1976	4.8	7.8	3.0	4.7	0.1
1977	6.8	8.4	1.6	6.6	0.2
1978	9.0	9.2	0.2	10.4	1.4
1979	13.3	10.6	—2.7	12.8	0.5
1980	12.4	12.4	0.0	16.5	4.1
1981	8.9	14.5	5.6	12.1	3.2
1982	3.9	11.2	7.3	8.5	4.6
1983	3.8	12.3	8.5	9.8	6.0
1984	4.0	12.0	8.0	8.2	4.0

play on this myth by advertising that next year the cost is going to go up. So what? God has obligated Himself to meet my needs always (see Phil. 4:19), and He didn't qualify that by saying "except for times of inflation."

The second thing that this myth presupposes, of course, is an increasing price; but there is example, after example, after example of the fallacy of sure increases, even during times of inflation. Ask any farmer how much his land has appreciated over the last few years. Yet just a few years ago, "everyone" knew that farm land would always go up because there is a limited supply of it. How about the price of oil? "Everyone"

Figure 5.2
REAL INTEREST RATES
1950–1984
(Market Rate Less Inflation Rate)

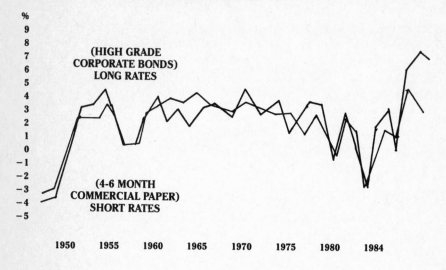

Reprinted from Johnson's Charts

knew that it would always go up because of the shortage of it. Or what about the price of foreign goods and electronic equipment? Or how about the price of beef? Even home prices in many areas of the country have leveled out and in many cases declined. Or what about mortgage rates? Those who purchased and mortgaged homes in 1983 at a 14% or 15% fixed rate because the rates would never go down are thinking differently today.

Be wary of the trap of buying anything because the price is going up in the future. Ask yourself first of all, Do I really need this? Second, if I do, but can't afford it, Has God promised to meet my needs? Of course He has, but not necessarily until you *really have a need*. He never seems to meet my needs in advance, but always right on time.

If you decide to fund your *greeds now* because of the possibility of future price increases, my advice is to do so with cash and never with borrowed money. Paying cash will cause you to make a better decision, and at least you will not have compounding working against you. You do, of course, experience the "opportunity cost of consumption" described in the last chapter.

Myth 2: Always Borrow to Buy

Two elements of truth support this myth: first of all, in times of inflation, the loan is paid back in cheaper dollars than those borrowed (because of the decline in purchasing power); and second, the tax deduction for interest expense makes the interest cost that much cheaper.

However, the myth has two presuppositions:

1. It presupposes a rate of interest that is less than the inflation rate, and a purchase that appreciates or earns more than the after-tax cost. In other words, it makes economic sense.
2. The cash or investment that could be used for the purchase is earning more than the cost of borrowing. Again, borrowing in that case makes economic sense.

These presuppositions are generally either ignored or not known. The guiding principle now seems to be: Always borrow because you need the interest expense for a tax deduction, and you will always be paying back with cheaper dollars.

To borrow money for the tax deduction is foolish. If you are in the 30% tax bracket, for every $100 spent on interest, you reduce your taxes by $30, *but* it cost you $100 to do so; therefore, you are out of pocket $70 ($100–$30). Spending more than what you save is hardly the way to achieve financial success, and yet this advice is given regularly, even by professionals who should know better.

It is true that in times of inflation you will be paying back borrowed dollars that are worth less than when you borrowed them. However, if you used the borrowed dollars to buy anything that depreciates in value, you have gained nothing financially by doing so and may have even lost in the whole transaction.

For example, let's assume that you borrow $12,000 on a 48-month loan at 12% in order to purchase a new car and that during this four-year-time period the inflation rate is 6% per year. For illustrative purposes, assume that the note is paid back at the end of the year and that the automobile you purchased has a value after four years of $4,000.
Are you now $2,880 more ahead financially than if you had not borrowed the money? Of course not, because the cost of $12,000, (the loan repayment) plus the interest cost of $3,600 ($1,440 + 1,080 + 720 + 360) gives a total cost of $15,600. This total cost is reduced by the "sav-

Chart 5–C

	Inflation "Savings"				Tax "Savings"				Total "Savings"
	Amount Owed	Ann. Infl. Rate			Annual Interest Cost	Tax Bracket			
Year 1	$12,000	× 6%	=	$ 720	$1,440	× 30%	=	$ 432	$1,152
Year 2	9,000	× 6%	=	540	1,080	× 30%	=	324	864
Year 3	6,000	× 6%	=	360	720	× 30%	=	216	576
Year 4	3,000	× 6%	=	180	360	× 30%	=	108	288
				$1,800 +				$1,080 =	$2,880

ings" of $2,880 and the remaining value of the car, $4,000, but you are now $8,720 behind where you started.

Had you not purchased the car, you would have kept the total payments of $15,600 but lost the inflation savings and tax savings of $2,880. You would have also lost the residual value of the car of $4,000 or the total of $8,720. That $8,720 could have been used to furnish transportation at a lesser cost or invested to grow to an even larger amount.

The point is that always borrowing to buy just because of inflation ignores the presuppositions mentioned on page 49. Using debt during times of inflation for leverage purposes can make sense, *but* only if these presuppositions are not ignored. In the next chapter we will take a close look at the leverage issue and the way leveraging has been distorted to justify funding whatever we want.

Myth 3: You Can Never Accumulate Enough

Understanding real interest rates and the magic of compounding is the key to destroying the myth that you can never accumulate enough to be protected from inflation during times of inflation. Incidentally, this myth is not a myth during times of hyperinflation if *all* of your assets are invested in money market instruments. (See Chapter 11 for how to protect yourself against this threat.)

First of all, this myth raises the question of what is "enough"? In my opinion, to accumulate enough means that I must have enough in an investment fund at retirement to generate enough income to live, give, and pay taxes. In other words, that investment fund must have sufficient "earning power."

In times of inflation, the earning power of investment funds will, over time, always be greater than the inflation rate, unless the investor ties his or her money up at a fixed rate of interest for a long term—which is foolishness in times of inflation.

A wise and knowledgeable person can beat inflation by spending less than is earned because the earning power of money will, over time, always be greater than the inflation rate. That earning power will even offset the required increase in income needed just to maintain a standard of living.

The myth that you can never accumulate enough prevails because there are many variables that enter in:

1. Time or the number of years until retirement.
2. The short-term goals, excluding children, accumulation needs, and mortgage payments. In other words, what could you live on if you did not have children to support, a mortgage payment, or the need to save?
3. Additional income from other sources at retirement.
4. The inflation rate.
5. The after-tax yield now and in the future.
6. Your current cash flow margin.
7. Current amount of investment funds.
8. Your personal inflation rate.

The effect of these variables may be seen in the formula below:

Illustration 5.1

1. Years until retirement	25
2. Estimated short-term goals need	$ 25,000
3. Less: Retirement income	$ (12,500)
Annual amount needed	$ 12,500
4. Inflation factor	6.0%
Future income needed (from Chart 5–A)	$ 53,625
5. Assumed after-tax yield ÷	10%
Investment fund needed	$ 536,250
6. Current investment fund	$ 25,000
Amount it will grow to (from Chart 4–B)	$(270,867)
Unfunded investment fund	$ 265,383
7. Annual cash flow margin needed (from Chart 4–C)	$ 2,453

The illustration assumes several things: The retirement income received from other sources will grow at least at the inflation rate; the ability to invest at after-tax yields will be considerably greater than the inflation rate; and the rate of inflation will not reach the level of hyperinflation. The illustration also ignores the impact of inflation on the investment fund at retirement when all the yield, which had been compounding, is being used to live on. Therefore, the "investment fund needed" is a minimum amount. The point is that if you are spending less than you earn, inflation can work for you rather than against you and you can fund enough. Even if you do not see how, God is still responsible to meet your needs and only requires that you take the first step of faith and obedience. In this case, that step is to generate a positive cash flow margin.

Myth 4: The Rate of Inflation Is Standard for Everyone

In personal financial planning, we figure for the impact of inflation by using the reported inflation rate. However, the reported national rate of inflation is an average and assumes that one makes significant purchases, such as a home, monthly. Such things just don't happen.

It has been my experience that when couples who plan to have a cash flow margin do so by living on some type of workable and simple budget, their personal rate of inflation is substantially less than the reported rate. They know what they spend and become price sensitive so that they are not victimized by inflation. On the other hand, if they have

Illustration 5.2

1. Years until retirement		25
2. Estimated short-term goals need		$ 25,000
3. Less: Retirement income		$ (12,500)
Annual amount needed		$ 12,500
4. Inflation factor		2%
Future income needed (from Chart 5–A)		$ 20,500
5. Assumed after-tax yield possible	÷	10%
Investment fund needed		$ 205,000
6. Current investment fund		$ 25,000
Amount it will grow to (from Chart 4–B)		$(270,867)
Unfunded (Overfunded) investment fund		$ (65,867)
7. Annual cash flow margin needed		$ –0–

THE MYTHS OF INFLATION   **53**

expenses over which they have no control, at the very least, they know how to pray specifically for God's intervention in the sure faith that God has committed to meet their needs.

To see the tremendous impact of a personal inflation rate that is less than the reported average annual inflation rate, assume that in our previous illustration the personal inflation factor is only 2% rather than the 6% national average.

The current investment fund grows to more than enough to meet the future income needs with *no* cash flow margin needed for the next 25 years.

The following formula is for your own personal example:

Illustration 5.3

1. Years until retirement $ _____
2. Estimated short-term goals need $ _____
3. Less: Retirement income $(_____)
      Annual amount needed $ _____
4. Inflation factor   _____%
      Future income needed (from Chart 5–A) $ _____
5. Assumed after-tax yield possible   ÷   _____%
      Investment fund needed $ _____
6. Current investment fund $ _____
      Amount it will grow to (from Chart 4–B) $(_____)
      Unfunded (Overfunded) investment fund $ _____
7. Annual cash flow margin needed (from Chart 4–C) $ _____

CONCLUSION

Inflation does not necessarily need to be feared. For those who are wise, knowledgeable, patient, self-disciplined and mature, it can work to their advantage.

In the last chapter, we raised the question of how much would $75,000,000 be worth in 40 years. In this chapter we implied that if we had a substantial level of inflation, you would end up with substantially more than $75,000,000 because the "real interest rate" will always be greater than the inflation rate.

We also demonstrated that the "earning power" of that $75,000,000 would be more than enough to provide for retirement.

If you are a lender of money rather than a borrower of money, you will beat inflation. In the next chapter we will look at the foolishness and devastation of being a borrower of money.

CHAPTER 6

The Dangers of Debt

THE FINANCIAL AREA of debt is clouded with more emotion, misunderstanding, and poor teaching than any other area, with the possible exceptions of life insurance and tithing. Before starting, we need to have a clear understanding of debt:

- Debt is not a sin! The Bible discourages the use of debt, but does not prohibit it.
- Debt is never the real problem, it is only symptomatic of the real problem—greed, self-indulgence, impatience, fear, poor self-image, lack of self-worth, lack of self-discipline, and perhaps many others.
- Debt can be defined many ways. I define it as "any money owed to anyone for anything."

There are five different kinds of debt: (1) credit card debt, (2) consumer debt, (3) mortgage debt, (4) investment debt, and (5) business debt.

In using any of the five kinds of debts, there are always four questions to ask:

1. Does it make economic sense?
2. Do my spouse and I have unity about taking on this debt?
3. Do I have the spiritual peace of mind or freedom to enter into this debt?
4. What personal goals and values am I meeting with this debt that can be met in *no* other way?

ECONOMIC DANGERS OF DEBT

The primary economic danger of debt is that compounding works against you rather than for you. For example, a 30-year mortgage on a home at a 10% interest rate requires that you pay back over three times the original amount borrowed.

Borrowed	$100,000
Interest rate	10%
Monthly payment	877.57
Months paid	×360
Total payments	$315,925

Or to restate the illustration used in the last chapter but in more current dollars, assume the following:

New car cost	$10,000.00
Monthly payment at 12.5%	265.80
Amount paid in four years	$12,758.40

Now, if you purchase another car in four years and again finance it and continue to do this over a working life of 40 years, you will have purchased 10 cars and paid in car payments $12,758.40 × 10 = $127,584. The bank received $265.80 per month for 480 months and never had at risk any more than $10,000; they in turn reinvested that $265.80 in other loans yielding 12.5%, so that they accumulated $3,641,550 on your total payments of $127,584. What if, instead of making car payments, you paid yourself $265.80 per month and were able to invest that payment at 12.5%, then *you* would have the $3,641,550, not the lending institution! $3,641,550 is the true cost of driving those cars, not $127,584!

Don't get me wrong. I am not against buying a new car, nor do I believe bankers are dishonest. (As a matter of fact, I used to own a major interest in two small banks.) But I am pointing out that consumption has a higher cost than many have ever realized. In Chapter 9, I will outline for you the most economical way to buy that new car, because many of us, myself included, enjoy driving a new car.

The second economic danger of debt is that debt becomes a trap—getting in takes no effort, but getting out can be next to impossible. In many cases, borrowing money can be no more difficult than signing your name or, at the most, filling out a lengthy form. Even borrowing the initial money for investments or starting a business can be almost effortless. It is so easy; it's like finding money lying on the street, and it gives a great feeling of satisfaction and power, at least momentarily.

The realization of the trap comes when the borrowed money must be paid back because by then the glamor has worn off whatever was purchased and the money used to repay the debt takes away the opportunity to buy other things. For example, assume that a couple overspends their income $1,000 each year for 10 years on impulsive purchases. Then realizing that they are $10,000 in debt, they decide to begin a program to get out of debt. By this point, not only are they overspending by $1,000 each year, but they are also paying at least $1,000 per year in interest (if the interest rate is only 10%).

Chart 6–A

	Overspending	Total Debt	Interest Paid
Year 1	$ 1,000	$ 1,000	$ 100
Year 2	1,000	2,000	200
Year 3	1,000	3,000	300
Year 4	1,000	4,000	400
Year 5	1,000	5,000	500
Year 6	1,000	6,000	600
Year 7	1,000	7,000	700
Year 8	1,000	8,000	800
Year 9	1,000	9,000	900
Year 10	1,000	10,000	1,000
Total	$10,000		$5,500

When they decide to get out of debt, first of all they must stop going into debt. Second, they must begin to pay back the accumulated debt and, all the while, continue to pay the interest. Their real costs are shown below.

Their total cost to overspend by $10,000 ($1,000 per year for 10 years) is $31,000. Notice that when they made their decision to get out of debt in year 10, their only cost was $1,000 per year in interest, but immediately after their decision in year 11, the effective cost went to $3,000, because they must forego in years 11 through 20 the overspend-

Chart 6–B

	Debt Repayment	Total Debt	Interest Paid
Year 11	$ 1,000	$9,000	$1,000
Year 12	1,000	8,000	900
Year 13	1,000	7,000	800
Year 14	1,000	6,000	700
Year 15	1,000	5,000	600
Year 16	1,000	4,000	500
Year 17	1,000	3,000	400
Year 18	1,000	2,000	300
Year 19	1,000	1,000	200
Year 20	1,000	–0–	100
Total	$10,000		$5,500

Chart 6–C

TRUE COST OF DEBT

	Overspending Reduction	Debt Repayment	Interest Paid	Total Cost
Year 1	0	0	$ 100	$ 100
Year 2	0	0	200	200
Year 3	0	0	300	300
Year 4	0	0	400	400
Year 5	0	0	500	500
Year 6	0	0	600	600
Year 7	0	0	700	700
Year 8	0	0	800	800
Year 9	0	0	900	900
Year 10	0	0	1,000	1,000
Year 11	$ 1,000	$ 1,000	1,000	3,000
Year 12	1,000	1,000	900	2,900
Year 13	1,000	1,000	800	2,800
Year 14	1,000	1,000	700	2,700
Year 15	1,000	1,000	600	2,600
Year 16	1,000	1,000	500	2,500
Year 17	1,000	1,000	400	2,400
Year 18	1,000	1,000	300	2,300
Year 19	1,000	1,000	200	2,200
Year 20	1,000	1,000	100	2,100
	$10,000	$10,000	$11,000	$31,000

ing formerly done in years 1 through 10. Just think—$21,000 that could have been used in far more productive and fun ways!

In Chapter 2, I said that "financial maturity is giving up today's desires for future benefits." Also, "the longer term the perspective, the better the financial decision is likely to be." Chart 6–C dramatically depicts these two principles.

There is another cost which is not so apparent; that is the income tax consequences. For example, in year 11, not only must they earn the $3,000 cost, but they must also earn the taxes on that $3,000 in order to have $3,000 left to pay the lender.

Income	$4,000
Taxes at 25%	1,000
Balance available	$3,000

They must earn $4,000 in order to have $3,000 left. There is, of course, a tax benefit of $250 to the interest paid ($1,000 tax deduction × 25% tax benefit). Therefore, they only need to earn $3,750 in order to have enough left over to fund their overspending, plus debt repayment, plus interest.

Getting in debt is as easy as getting down an ice-covered mountain. Getting out of debt is just as difficult as climbing that same mountain.

The third economic danger to debt is that debt always mortgages the future. The first priority use of future income must be debt repayment—not giving or lifestyle or investing or even taxes! The freedom of choice disappears. The consequences of debt are a paradox.

Current marketplace wisdom says to you, "Raise your standard of living by buying what you want and pay for it while you enjoy it," but the reality is that you may be sentencing yourself to a lower standard of living in the future. Look again at Chart 6–C.

This couple enjoyed themselves to the tune of $1,000 per year beyond their income in the first 10 years, but their second 10 years was being mortgaged and resulted in a *much* greater cost than the earlier benefit. The paradox is that while seeming to raise their standard of living, they were in reality, over the long term, lowering it. What a deception! This illustration may portray why so many couples go through some very difficult times or divorce after 8–12 years of marriage.

SPIRITUAL DANGERS OF DEBT

The spiritual dangers of borrowing money are twofold: First of all, borrowing *always* presumes upon the future and, second, borrowing *may* deny God an opportunity to work.

The Bible definitely warns us about presuming upon the future. In James 4:16, presuming upon the future is called "arrogance." In Luke 14:28, Jesus said: "For which of you, intending to build a tower, does not sit down first and count the cost, whether he has enough to finish it?" Whenever any money is borrowed for any purpose, there is a presumption of repayment. In fact, from the lender's viewpoint it is not only a presumption, it is a certainty.

A friend and I were discussing the biblical admonition against presuming upon the future and the requirement that whenever a Christian borrows money, it must be paid back. Psalm 37:21 says in part, "The wicked borrows and does not repay." We concluded that many Christians in America may be counting on the Rapture to get them out of debt. He said to me, "Wouldn't it be something if, when Jesus came back to rapture the church, He left all the Christians who had debt of any kind here on earth to repay it rather than taking them to heaven?" Both of us became quiet and then he said, "You know, maybe the Rapture has already occurred!"

An obvious biblical financial principle flows out of that truth.

> *Whenever you borrow money for any reason, there must be a* **guaranteed** *way to pay it back.*

Not a "hoped-for" way, such as an increase in income nor even the continuation of income, but a guaranteed way *regardless* of the circumstances. If this principle were followed, there would be almost no risk to debt. Not to have a guaranteed way to repay is *always* to presume upon the future.

The second spiritual danger of debt is that it *may* deny God an opportunity to work.

Over the years I have started several businesses of my own and have had the privilege of counseling many hundreds of others who have been in the initial stages of founding their own businesses. One of the things that is standard in starting a business is to secure from a bank a line of credit or some terms of financing so there is always cash available to meet the unexpected needs of a new business. Therefore, when I started this business in the fall of 1979, I went to the bank and arranged for a line of credit.

In the following weeks, as I prayed through the many issues regard-ing the starting of this business, I felt less and less comfortable with having borrowed to start this business, even though it made "good sense." Eventually, I felt so strongly convicted about the need not to have debt that I called the bank and canceled my line of credit. This was an extremely risky thing to do, as I had a totally unproven business, no clients, and very little financial resources personally.

Approximately one week after I canceled the line of credit, I was visiting in the training department of a major international corporation headquartered in Atlanta. During the conversation with one of the training directors, he asked me if I had any interest in developing a financial planning seminar for his organization. As a matter of fact, I had been in the process at that very time of developing a financial planning seminar in order to provide a conceptual framework for the financial planning process. Of course, I said, "Yes." He then asked me how much I would charge them to develop such a seminar. I had no idea what large corporations paid for such work, so I simply asked, "What would you pay?"

He thought for a moment before saying they would pay me $6,000 to develop the seminar and another $4,000 if I would teach it four times during the next year—a total of $10,000. Coincidentally, the line of credit I had arranged at the bank was for $10,000. Of course, I replied that $10,000 for that work sounded "very fair." He also asked me if they could go ahead and pay me the $6,000 immediately in order to get it into the current year's budget. With no hesitation I gave him my address.

I am convinced that had I not canceled the line of credit with the bank and depended solely upon God to provide the resources, I never would have received the contract to design the seminar. I am convinced that had I borrowed the money, the training director would never have made the offer he did, because to this day I can take no credit for having received the money. God provided it in an unusual, undeniable, and supernatural fashion!

I believe that in many cases, when we borrow the money to fund one item, be it for the purpose of a new car, a television, a new home, a vacation, or whatever, we are putting the lender in the place of God. Who needs God to provide for us if someone will lend to us?

We seem to be very unwilling to wait for God's timing and for God's method to meet our needs and our desires. We prefer to have it done our way, on our timing. Yet, Isaiah 55:8–9 says, " 'For My thoughts are not your thoughts, / Nor are your ways My ways,' says the LORD. / 'For as the heavens are higher than the earth, / So are My ways higher than your ways, / And My thoughts than your thoughts.' " Invariably, God's method of meeting my needs and desires is different from my method. The question that we need to ask ourselves is, "Does God provide for what I want by providing borrowed funds, or is this me meeting my needs and desires in my own way?"

BIBLICAL PRINCIPLES OF BORROWING

In addition to presuming upon the future and potentially denying God an opportunity to work, there are many other biblical principles relative to debt and borrowing. In Psalm 37:21 we read, "The wicked borrows and does not repay, / But the righteous shows mercy and gives." The principle that comes from this verse is that not repaying debt is never an option for the Christian, but this verse also implies that a righteous person is able to give rather than borrow. I personally do not believe that financial success is necessarily symptomatic of righteousness. If we equate righteousness and financial success, many evil people could be defined as righteous. All of us have seen too many examples to the contrary.

Romans 13:8 says, "Owe no one anything except to love one another, for he who loves another has fulfilled the law." The context of this passage does not deal with finances. (Even if it were on finances, I do not believe that it specifically prohibits debt.) What it does do, however, is set up a principle that says, "If I owe anyone anything, I am not free to give love to that person." Anyone who has borrowed money from another person, and especially another Christian, realizes the wall that immediately goes up from being in a debtor/lender relationship. Debtors and lenders are not really free to love one another. This verse suggests principles for both sides. Lending to another Christian needs to be considered very, very seriously before it is done. On the other side, before you borrow from anyone for anything, consider the ramifications of being in bondage to that person. Are you, in fact, free to love that person?

Proverbs 22:7 says, "The rich rules over the poor, / And the borrower is servant to the lender." Anyone who has borrowed or been in bondage to debt knows the truth of this verse. The reality is that whenever you have borrowed from anyone, you are a servant to that person. This verse does not prohibit debt, of course, but it certainly cautions against the use of debt. We could say that anyone who uses debt for any purpose, at the very least, is not using biblical wisdom and, in fact, may be a "fool." Again, a great caution, but not a prohibition, against debt.

First Timothy 5:8 says, "But if anyone does not provide for his own, and especially for those of his household, he has denied the faith and is worse than an unbeliever." The underlying biblical principle relative to debt in this verse is that by taking on debt you may run the risk of not providing for your own. Because debt mortgages the future and because the negative compounding of debt works against you, you may very well end up in the future not providing for your own. Therefore, this verse says that you have denied the faith and are worse than an unbeliever. Obviously, the danger is great and needs to be avoided.

Luke 12:15 says, "Take heed and beware of covetousness, for one's life does not consist in the abundance of the things he possesses." The caution in this verse is clear: "Beware, and be on your guard against *every form of greed.*" Debt makes it very easy to fund greeds; yet in doing so, we may violate the biblical principle set forth in this verse. As I said earlier, the question to ask is, "Am I funding my *needs* or my *greeds*?"

In the book of Proverbs much is said about "surety" and the foolishness of going surety. Surety in itself is not debt, but it is rather guaranteeing the debt of another. To be a surety on any debt is violation of a definite biblical principle. Many people equate surety and debt, and they are the same in the sense that both are obligations to debt.

The Bible contains many other passages dealing with money and specifically with debt. We need to ask ourselves, "Why is so much written about debt in God's Word?" I believe there are three reasons. First of all, debt is extremely deceptive. As we said earlier, getting into debt is easy—getting out is next to impossible. Second, debt creates bondage, and if that bondage is to the world system, we are no longer free to be the witnesses in this world that God has called us to be. Third, debt is almost blasphemous when we use it and deny God an opportunity to work. With all of these cautions and warnings against debt, I still believe that in some cases debt is acceptable, but only under certain conditions.

CRITERIA FOR UNDERTAKING ANY DEBT

First of all, does it make economic sense to incur the debt? To determine this, there are two rules to follow:

- The cost to borrow (after-tax interest) must be *less than* the economic benefit received (interest, yield, and/or growth in value).
- There must be a *guaranteed* way of repayment.

Second, are *both* spouses free from any anxiety regarding this debt? The rule indicates that there must be unity between the spouses.

Third, can the debt be undertaken with spiritual peace of mind? The rule is that if I experience any lack of peace when I picture myself taking on this debt, I do not enter into the debt.

Fourth, I ask myself, what personal goals and values am I meeting with this debt that can be met in *no* other way?

I believe these criteria are practical, pragmatic, and biblical and should be applied unemotionally to every debt opportunity. They leave us with the following conclusions as we apply them to the five kinds of debt:

1. *Credit card debt.* It will never satisfy the economic criteria and, therefore, should never be used. Using credit cards, which always have a high interest rate, to accumulate the consumptive and depreciating items makes no sense economically. Whether or not to use credit cards for convenience will be addressed in Chapter 9.

2. *Consumer debt.* Consumer debt is debt that is used to finance cars, furniture, vacations and other consumptive and depreciating items. It is exactly like credit card debt except that the process of applying for it can be more lengthy. Because it is just like credit card debt, it should be avoided at all costs.

Both credit card debt and consumer debt are to be avoided, I believe, not because they are sinful in themselves, unless they are being used to satisfy greed (see Luke 12:15), but because they just don't make sense economically. The only exception (and I do *not* have an example or illustration of this) would be using them for a personal goal and value that could be met in no other way, a personal goal and value that unquestionably came from God. Implicitly, this says that God has chosen debt to meet a personal need. Again, I have never seen an example of this, but I would not want to put God into a box and say that He could never do it.

3. *Mortgage debt.* We Americans have come to believe that owning a home is a God-given right. We have trained our children to expect to begin their married life in a home it took our parents a lifetime to save for! Additionally, during the last 35 to 40 years, and especially the years 1960 to 1980, a home purchased with a fixed interest rate was the safest and surest way to build personal net worth and equity. Beginning in 1983, however, the "rules of the game" changed; inflation slowed down and interest rates went up—a direct reversal of these two factors from the previous twenty years. It has taken a while for our society to recognize this, and I don't believe we have, as yet, accepted it.

When considering the purchase of a home, we should apply the same four criteria as for undertaking any debt. However, the economic criteria are very difficult to nail down in today's economic environment. Even in the period 1960 to 1980, there was not a guaranteed way to pay the debt except for returning the home back to the lending institution. My counsel to young couples who are considering the purchase of a home is never to become so attached to the home that they could not give it up if the debt could not be paid. Jobs are not nearly as secure today as they were in the past. Inflation is certainly not a sure thing, and fixed low interest rates may very well be a thing of the past.

The psychological burden of home mortgage debt is more severe than most people think, especially if a woman whose center of influence and security is in her home is involved. Studies have shown that having mortgage debt is a stressful factor and that the degree of stress relates to the amount of the mortgage.

The question of whether or not to pay off the mortgage, if that is an option, is really an economic, psychological, and spiritual decision. Economically, it may not make sense to pay off a low interest rate mortgage, even if one has the funds to do so. However, psychologically and spiritually, it may be, by far, the best course. Again, I would remind you that finances are nothing more than a resource to accomplish other goals and objectives—they are never an end in themselves. Therefore, even if it does not make economic sense to pay off a mortgage, there may be higher priority goals and objectives that need to be met. Money then becomes merely the resource to meet those goals. The decision does not have to be always an economic one. That counsel is, of course, good for all decisions.

4. *Investment and business debt.* The order of applying the four basic criteria for any debt is a good one before taking on investment or business debt. Let me repeat the criteria here: Is the rate of return greater

VULNERABILITY OF STRESS SCALE

Psychiatrist Thomas H. Holmes and his colleagues at the University of Washington School of Medicine have developed a scale to measure the relative stress induced by various changes in a person's life. The amount of stress is measured on a point scale of 200 "life-change units." Studies by Dr. Holmes and his associates show that if you accumulate more than 300 units in a single year, your life has probably been disrupted enough to make you vulnerable to illness.

EVENT	SCALE OF IMPACT
Death of Spouse	100
Divorce	73
Marital separation	65
Jail term	63
Death of close family member	63
Personal injury or illness	53
Marriage	50
Fired at work	47
Marital reconciliation	45
Retirement	45
Change in health of family member	44
Pregnancy	40
Sex difficulties	39
Gain of new family member	39
Business readjustment	39
Change in financial state	38
Death of close friend	37
Change to different line of work	36
Change in number of arguments with spouse	35
Mortgage over $10,000	31
Foreclosure of mortgage or loan	30
Change in responsibilities at work	29
Son or daughter leaving home	29
Trouble with in-laws	29
Outstanding personal achievement	28
Wife begins or stops work	26
Begin or end school	26
Change in living conditions	25
Revision of personal habits	24
Trouble with boss	23
Change in work hours or conditions	20
Change in residence	20
Change in recreation	19
Change in church activities	19
Change in social activities	18
Mortgage or loan less than $10,000	17

Change in sleeping habits	16
Change in number of family get-togethers	15
Change in eating habits	15
Vacation	13
Christmas	12
Minor violation of the law	11

than the cost, both on an after-tax basis? Is there a guaranteed way to repay the debt? Are both spouses in perfect agreement and unity? And do you have spiritual peace of mind when considering this debt?

My experience has been that no business opportunity or investment opportunity ever comes packaged as anything other than "a good deal." I probably see a thousand "good deals" a year. No one has ever come to the office or sent a proposal and said, "Let me show you a bad deal." On the front end, every business and investment deal is a good one. It only went bad later! What makes investment and business debts so difficult to evaluate and reject are that they are all presented as good deals, and a person would be foolish to turn them down. Therefore, there never seems to be economic justification alone for turning them down.

This is one of the reasons why I feel it is so important to apply the rule that a husband and wife have perfect unity on their debt decisions. God has granted to women a special sense, which some have called intuition, that cannot be explained, but in many cases, it has kept a husband from making a poor decision.

I remember speaking one time to a group of professional athletes, and as I related that principle with them, one of the wives sat with tears streaming down her cheeks. Afterward she shared with me how her husband, who had played on three Super Bowl championship teams, had been presented with a business opportunity that was a "sure thing." Against his wife's counsel, he had mortgaged everything, gone into the business and had eventually lost all they owned. What does a forty-year-old ex-athlete with no training or money and a family do? It was a tragic, yet typical, case.

I give two general rules in this area. First of all, if you cannot explain the deal or investment to your wife in such a way that she totally understands it, don't do it. Second, even if you can explain it so that she totally understands it, but she feels uneasy or unsure in any way about it, don't do it. Granted, you may pass up many opportunities. However, one of the surest ways to financial success is to avoid the major mistakes, because not only do you have to make up for the lost investment, but also you lose the earnings that this money could have generated, and the earnings that the earnings could have generated, and the earnings that the earnings that the earnings could have generated, and so on. Again, the biblical counsel is sound: "He who gathers money little by little makes it grow." Or as we have stated in the previous chapter, "Get rich slow."

Again, let me say, debt is not a sin. The Bible discourages the use of debt, but does not prohibit it. Being in debt is never the real problem; it is only symptomatic of the real problem, which is usually greed, self-indulgence, impatience, fear, a poor self-image, lack of self-discipline, and perhaps others. So, if you find yourself in debt, your first question is not, "How do I get out of debt?" Ask first of all, "Why am I in this situation?" and answer that question. Then getting out of debt will become much easier. The best way to get out of debt is, first of all, to stop going into debt, and then second, to set up some type of repayment plan.

Please understand that I am not being judgmental, because I know better than most the temptation that debt presents.

My heart goes out to the many young couples, and even older couples, whom I have visited and who will suffer under the burden of debt for many years to come. But they must recognize the problem that caused the debt and then, as Proverbs 3:5–6 says, "Trust in the LORD with all your heart, / And lean not on your own understanding; / In all your ways acknowledge Him, / And He shall direct your paths." God is faithful and will provide a way.

CHAPTER 7

Where Am I?

WE HAVE LOOKED at many principles and concepts. By way of review, we have defined stewardship as "The use of God-given resources for the accomplishment of God-given goals," and planning as "The allocation of limited resources to unlimited alternatives." We have also reviewed the magic of compounding and concluded that a dollar spent today takes multiple dollars out of the future or a dollar saved today puts multiple dollars into the future.

We then looked at the concept of margin and concluded that there was only one way to achieve financial freedom and success, and that was to spend less than you earn and do it over a long time period. In the last chapter, we examined the kinds of debt and the four criteria to apply before taking on debt. Now we are ready to put these principles and concepts into practical application—to answer the question, Where am I?

When I ask someone how they are doing financially, they typically respond by telling me what their income is or by telling me about their most recent expensive purchase. In reality, neither may be of importance in describing financial health. To know conclusively where you are financially is necessary before you can even begin to plan for the accomplishment of goals, dreams, and desires.

The financial planning diagram on page 70 depicts four steps to financial planning. *Step 1:* "Summarize Present Situation," will be covered in this chapter and basically answers the question, Where am I? *Step 2:* "Establish Financial Goals," will be covered in the next chapter and answers the question, Where do I want to go? And *Steps 3* and *4:* "Increase Cash Flow Margin" and "Control Cash Flow" answer the question, How

Figure 7.1

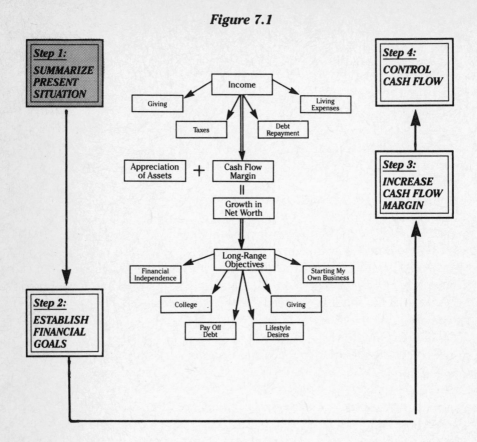

do I get to where I want to go from where I am? and will be covered in Chapters 9–13.

Before you move from Step 1 to Step 2, you need to analyze where you are relative to where you want to go. Three financial summaries will give you the necessary facts:

- Statement of net worth
- Summary of cash flow
- Summary of life insurance coverage

STATEMENT OF NET WORTH

A statement of net worth is much like a snapshot or x-ray. It gives a summary of every financial decision that has been made, but it summarizes those financial transactions at a specific point in time. Specifically, a statement of net worth lists all of the assets that are owned, then subtracts from that listing of assets all of the liabilities, or debts owed; and the resulting number totals one's net worth.

Over time, my five children have learned that by performing odd jobs, part-time or full-time jobs, they can earn money. For the most part, that money has been spent on personal needs and desires and, therefore, the accumulation has not been very great; but at least there has been some accumulation.

In typical fashion, they will complete college and find that their income does not support their needs. Therefore, they will borrow to fund some of their desires and needs—an automobile, some furniture, a home, and maybe even further education. If they add up what they have accumulated in the way of cash, investments, furniture, cars, homes, etc., they will have the total of all they own. However, they may have a substantial amount of debt which, when subtracted from what they own, would leave a small or even a negative net worth situation.

At any point anyone can add up his or her assets, subtract liabilities, and get a picture of the net worth. This one number is a summary of every financial transaction ever entered into. The objective, of course, is to have that number growing in size relative to life's goals and objectives as a whole.

The value of the net worth statement becomes clear when you examine the finances of Bob and Laura, a fictitious, but very typical couple. They have been married for 10 years, have two children, and face some major questions in their financial life such as how much to give, where to give, how to reduce taxes, how much life insurance to own, whether to participate in the company savings plan, how to reduce their debt, what investments make sense for them now, etc. To help begin the analysis, their assets and liabilities are listed and categorized as follows:

Chart 7–A

Bob and Laura
ASSETS

LIQUID:

Cash on hand and checking account .... $ 2,000
Money market funds ....   –0–
CD's (interest rate _____%) ....   –0–

Savings (6% interest rate)	5,000
Marketable securities	5,000
Life insurance cash values	6,000
_____	–0–
_____	–0–
Total liquid assets	$ 18,000

NONLIQUID:

Home (market value)	$ 80,000
Land (market value)	5,000
Business valuation	–0–
Real estate investments	15,000
Limited partnerships	–0–
Boat, camper, tractor, etc.	6,000
Automobile(s) (market value)	8,000
Furniture and personal property (estimated market value)	5,000
Coin & stamp collections, antiques	–0–
IRA's	–0–
Pension & profit-sharing	–0–
Receivables from others	–0–
_____	–0–
Total nonliquid assets	$119,000

Chart 7–B

Bob and Laura
LIABILITIES

	Balance	Interest	Payment Schedule	
Creditor	Due	Rate	Per Month	Until When
1. Charge Cards	$ 1,000	18%	$ 50	Forever
2. Furniture Loans	1,000	18%	50	2 Years
3. Auto Loans	4,000	12%	150	4 Years
4. Parents	5,000	6%	—	?
5. Boat Loan	5,000	14%	200	3 Years
6. Bank Loan	5,000	15%	200	10 Years
7. Life Insurance	5,000	5%	—	?
8. Home Mortgage	40,000	8%	290	25 Years
9.				
10.				
Totals	$66,000		$940	

We asked them to list their assets at a value they could be sold for and their liabilities at the current balance due. To come up with their net worth, we subtracted the total balance owed of $66,000 from the total of liquid and nonliquid assets of $71,000 and showed them that they now have a net worth of $62,500. So what does this mean?

It means that they have some problems in their financial situation, which they may or may not have recognized. They have some strengths, which could be used to their advantage; they also need to take some action. We analyzed their statement of net worth as follows:

Chart 7–C

Bob and Laura
PERSONAL BALANCE SHEET ANALYSIS

1. NET WORTH

Assets		
Liquid	$ 18,000	
Nonliquid	119,000	
TOTAL	137,000	
Less: Total Liabilities	(66,000)	
Net Worth	$ 71,000	

2. LIQUIDITY

   (For emergencies, bills, major purchases, and investment opportunities) $18,000

3. PRODUCTIVE ASSETS

	Liquid Assets	18,000	$38,000
	Real Estate	15,000	
	Land	5,000	

   (Generating or having the potential to generate income)

4. PROPENSITY TO BORROW $\quad \dfrac{66,000}{137,000} \quad = \quad$ 48%

   (Liabilities divided by assets)

5. PROPENSITY TO ACCUMULATE $\quad \dfrac{71,000}{10 \text{ years}} \quad = \quad$ $7,100/year

   (Net worth divided by years worked)

Liquid Assets

When preparing the statement of net worth, one major category of assets is those that are liquid—in other words, those assets that could be converted into cash immediately with no loss of principal. The person who has liquidity says, "I have financial flexibility in order to meet emergencies, unexpected bills, make major purchases, and take advantage of opportunities that come along." Obviously, the more liquid the finances, the more flexible the person is—and probably more financially secure.

Our grandparents put most of their money in the bank because it was relatively safe and totally liquid. They had greater flexibility in their financial situation and greater security. However, there is a risk to having all of one's resources in the bank or invested in cash or cash-type investments. These risks will be covered in Chapter 13, "Investment Planning."

Productive Assets

The next category of assets on the net worth statement includes those that are productive as opposed to those that are basically passive in nature. A productive asset generates or has the potential to generate income for investment purposes. Bob and Laura's listing of productive assets includes all of the liquid assets plus the investment land and real estate investments, for a total of $38,000. Some of their other assets may grow in value, such as their home, but that was not their primary reason for purchasing a home. The purpose of the home is to have a place to live, and it is typically not sold merely to produce income.

In comparing Bob and Laura's total productive assets of $38,000 to their total assets of $137,000, a rather typical picture emerges of a young couple who has invested, over time, their excess cash flow for the most part in personal-type assets as opposed to investment assets or productive assets. If Bob and Laura continue to follow the usual pattern as they grow older, the amount of their productive assets will grow in relation to their total assets because accumulation needs are generally met sometime between the ages of 35 and 50. After that point, the primary emphasis is on accumulating assets that can be used to fund retirement when it comes. Thus, such assets are also more productive in nature than cars, boats, homes, and so on.

Propensity to Borrow

Bob and Laura have a propensity to borrow—that is, their liabilities divided by their assets reveal they are 48% likely to borrow in order to accumulate. In other words, 48% of their assets have been accumulated by borrowing rather than by generating a positive cash flow margin. (The lower the percentage of borrowing to accumulate, the better the financial situation is. Zero percent means that there has been no borrowing to accumulate; 100% or greater means that there has been no excess cash flow and that all assets have been accumulated by borrowing. It also means that this person or couple is bankrupt and could not meet their debts even if they sold everything.)

The propensity to borrow is a ratio that I have used in my financial analysis of other people's situations, merely to point out that accumulation of things is not the objective. That can be done through borrowed funds in many cases, but it does not mean that just because there are many things accumulated, one has a secure financial situation. Debt against those things means that in reality they are not owned by the one who has them, but rather by the lender. As the biblical principle states: The borrower becomes the lender's slave.

Propensity to Accumulate

Another measurement I use in doing a financial analysis is the propensity to accumulate, which is calculated by dividing net worth by the number of years worked. It is merely an indicator of how much accumulation on the average has taken place each year. It also indicates where that couple might end up financially if they continued at that rate of accumulation.

For example, Bob and Laura's net worth of $71,000 divided by 10, the number of years that Bob has worked, means that they have been able to accumulate, on the average, $7,100 per year. If Bob still has 30 years of productivity left, and continues to accumulate at $7,100 per year, he will end up at retirement with a net worth of $284,000. However, if that amount of $7,100 can be compounded at a reasonable investment rate, they will have accumulated substantially more than $284,000. They are making progress toward the accomplishment of their long-term goals.

There is no right level for the propensity to accumulate because it depends upon the long-term goals, but the higher it is, the sooner you will achieve these long-term goals. Working through mathematically the propensity to borrow and the propensity to accumulate points out that the higher the debt ratio or propensity to borrow, the lower the propensity to accumulate. In other words, borrowing does not always help you to achieve your financial goals and objectives.

During the very first seminar on financial planning that I taught, an older couple was preparing their statement of net worth. I heard the wife say to the husband, "I didn't know we owned that," and a little bit later, "When did we buy that?" and somewhat later, "Why do we have that debt?" In talking with them later, I learned that the two of them had never prepared a statement of net worth together, and only the husband knew approximately where they stood financially. I have subsequently found that this is very common—that a husband and wife very rarely sit down and discuss where they are financially by looking at an actual statement of their net worth. I absolutely advise every couple to annually prepare and review a statement of net worth.

Pointers in Preparing a Statement of Net Worth

You can use the forms on pages 77–78 of this book to complete and analyze your own statement of net worth. Some pointers in preparing such a statement are:

1. You should remember that a liquid asset is one that can be converted to cash immediately.
2. You should use estimates of the market value.
3. Where market values are not known, you should use the original cost value.
4. You should not list the net values of investments and real estate owned since the liability will be listed under the liabilities section.
5. You should consider stocks and bonds as marketable securities.
6. You should list Individual Retirement Accounts under nonliquid assets because there is a penalty for withdrawing these funds prematurely.
7. You should include pension and profit-sharing accounts only if the fund is actually yours and could be taken with you or liquidated at your choice. List pension and retirement plans as nonliquid assets only if you have the right to withdraw them without penalty. (In other words, they are assets that you have funded personally and

not a company-funded contribution, which will be taxed if with-drawn prematurely.)

8. In listing your debts, you may want to list long-term debts first—for example, the home mortgage.

9. You should not include utility bills and monthly bills as a liability since these will be covered under the cash flow summary. If you are behind on your utility payments or monthly bills, list the amount you are in arrears as a debt that is due.

Chart 7–D

YOUR ASSETS

<u>LIQUID:</u>

Cash on hand and checking account . . . . $_____
Money market funds . . . . _____
CD's (interest rate _____%) . . . . _____
Savings (6% interest rate) . . . . _____
Marketable securities . . . . _____
Life insurance cash values . . . . _____
_____ . . . . _____
_____ . . . . _____

             Total liquid assets . . . . $_____

<u>NONLIQUID:</u>

Home . . . . $_____
Land . . . . _____
Business valuation . . . . _____
Real estate investments . . . . _____
Limited partnerships . . . . _____
Boat, camper, tractor, etc. . . . . _____
Automobile(s) (market value) . . . . _____
Furniture and personal property
   (estimated market value) . . . . _____
Coin & stamp collections, antiques . . . . _____
IRA's . . . . _____
Pension & profit-sharing . . . . _____
Receivables from others . . . . _____
_____ . . . . _____

             Total nonliquid assets . . . . $_____

Chart 7–E

YOUR PERSONAL BALANCE SHEET ANALYSIS

1. <u>NET WORTH</u>

   Assets
   Liquid $ _____
   Nonliquid   _____
   TOTAL   _____
   Less: Total Liabilities   (_____)
      Net Worth $ _____

2. <u>LIQUIDITY</u> $ _____

   (For emergencies, bills, major purchases, and investment opportunities)

3. <u>PRODUCTIVE ASSETS</u> $ _____

   (Generating or having the potential to generate income)

4. <u>PROPENSITY TO BORROW</u>   _____ %

   (Liabilities divided by assets)

5. <u>PROPENSITY TO ACCUMULATE</u> $ _____

   (Net worth divided by years worked)

SUMMARY OF CASH FLOW

If the statement of net worth can be compared to a snapshot or an x-ray, then the summary of cash flow can be likened to a movie. Cash flow is not a measurement at a point in time like a net worth statement, but is rather a measurement of cash inflows and cash outflows over a defined period. Cash flow is either retrospective, a summary of what has happened over a period of time in the past, or it is prospective, a projection of what is going to happen over a period of time in the future.

Review again the financial planning diagram on page 70 and notice that there are six elements to cash flow. First there is the inflow, which comes from salary, business income, earnings or investments, and pension retirement income; and then there are five outflows: giving, taxes, debt repayment, living expenses, and accumulation.

Cash Flow

We can examine the cash flow for Bob and Laura in five steps:

1. by projecting their income in Exhibit A (shown below);
2. by projecting their giving for the next 12-month time period in Exhibit B (see page 80);
3. by projecting their taxes for all types of taxes in Exhibit C (see page 80);
4. by projecting their debt repayment in Exhibit D (see page 81); and
5. by projecting their living expenses over the next 12 months, in Exhibit E (see pages 82–83).

Chart 7–F

**Bob and Laura
EXHIBIT A
PROJECTED INCOME**

SOURCES		Amount Received Monthly	Amount Received Other Than Monthly	Total Annual Amount
Gross Wages—Husband		$2,500	$ —	$30,000
Gross Wages—Wife			2,000	2,000
Dividends	Marketable Securities		300	300
Dividends				
Dividends				
Interest	Savings		300	300
Interest				
Interest				
Rents				
Business				
Pensions and Annuities				
Other	Real Estate Investment		2,000	2,000
Other				
Other				
	Total Gross Income	$2,500	$4,600	$34,600

Chart 7–G

Bob and Laura
EXHIBIT B
GIVING

GIVING	Organization	Monthly	Annual	Total
Church		$100	$	$1,200
Other	Christian organ. (A)	50		600
Other	Christian organ. (B)		400	400
Other				
Other				
Other				
Other				
Other				
Other				
Other				
Other				
Other				
	Total	$150	$400	$2,200

Chart 7–H

Bob and Laura
EXHIBIT C
TAXES SUMMARY

DEDUCTIONS, WITHHOLDINGS, AND ESTIMATES	Monthly Withholdings	Quarterly Estimates	Total Paid Annually
Federal Income Tax	$520	$ 0	$6,240
State and City Income Tax	115	0	1,380
Social Security Tax	181	0	2,172
Total Tax	$816	$ 0	$9,792

To review Bob and Laura's situation, their projected income (from Exhibit A) over the next 12 months is $2,500 per month from salaries and then $4,600, which is not received on a monthly basis for a total annual amount of $34,600, which by itself looks pretty good. However, this is without considering the outflow.

You should also note that it was necessary to prepare the statement of net worth *first* in order not to miss the income from such things as dividends on marketable securities, interest on the savings account and the real estate investment, which generates a cash flow of $2,000 per year. In addition to salaries and wages, dividends, interest, etc., there may be sales of assets, pension plan liquidations, and commissions. Commissions are difficult to project because they are unknown. My recommendation is that couples project commission income on a conservative basis as they estimate a projected cash flow.

Giving

The giving amounts from Exhibit B are again of two types: those that are given on a normal monthly basis, and those that are given on some other basis, such as annually, as a result of an appeal or pledge that has been made previously. The total indicates that Bob and Laura are projecting to give $2,200 for the next year.

Taxes

The tax summary that is projected for Bob and Laura includes all income taxes and Social Security taxes, but not property taxes or other

Chart 7–I

Bob and Laura
EXHIBIT D
DEBT REPAYMENT

			Payment Schedule	
Creditor	Balance Due	Interest Rate	Per Month	Until When
1. Charge Cards	$ 1,000	18%	$ 50	Forever
2. Furniture Loans	1,000	18%	50	2 Years
3. Auto Loans	4,000	12%	150	4 Years
4. Parents	5,000	6%	—	?
5. Boat Loan	5,000	14%	200	3 Years
6. Bank Loan	5,000	15%	200	10 Years
7. Life Insurance	5,000	5%	—	?
8.				
9.				
10.				
Totals	$26,000		$650	

types of taxes. The information with which to prepare this summary came from their pay stubs. In addition to the deductions and withholdings, a person might be subject to tax estimates, which are paid on a quarterly basis. In the case of Bob and Laura, they are paying a total of $816 per month of tax withholdings or $9,792 on an annual basis.

Chart 7–J

Bob and Laura
EXHIBIT E
LIVING EXPENSES
Year:

	Amount Paid Monthly	Amount Paid Other Than Monthly	Total Annual Amount
HOUSING			
Mortgage/rent	$ 290	$	$ 3,480
Insurance	—	400	400
Property taxes	—	1,000	1,000
Electricity	60		720
Heating	40		480
Water	30		360
Sanitation	—		—
Telephone	40		480
Cleaning	—		—
Repairs/maintenance	20		240
Supplies	10		120
Improvements	—		—
Furnishings	50		600
Total Housing	$ 540	$1,400	$ 7,880
FOOD	$ 400	$	$ 4,800
CLOTHING	$ —	$1,000	$ 1,000
TRANSPORTATION			
Insurance	$ —	$ 500	$ 500
Gas and oil	150		1,800
Maintenance/repairs	30		360
Parking			
Other			
Total Transportation	$ 180	$ 500	$ 2,660

EXHIBIT E (continued)

	Amount Paid Monthly	Amount Paid Other Than Monthly	Total Annual Amount
ENTERTAINMENT/RECREATION			
Eating Out	$ 40	$	$ 480
Babysitters	10		120
Magazines/newspapers	20		240
Vacation		1,000	1,000
Clubs and activities		300	300
Total Entertain/Rec.	$ 70	$1,300	$ 2,140
MEDICAL EXPENSES			
Insurance	$ 60	$	$ 720
Doctors	20		240
Dentists	20		240
Drugs	5		60
Other			
Total Medical	$ 105	$	$ 1,260
INSURANCE			
Life	$ 128	$	$ 1,536
Disability			
Total Insurance	$ 128	$	$ 1,536
CHILDREN			
School lunches	$ 30	$	$ 360
Allowances	20		240
Tuition		2,400	2,400
Lessons	20		240
Other	5		60
Other	5		60
Total Children	$ 80	$2,400	$ 3,360
GIFTS			
Christmas	$	$ 500	$ 500
Birthdays		150	150
Anniversary		200	200
Other	25		300
Total Gifts	$ 25	$ 850	$ 1,150
MISCELLANEOUS			
Toiletries	$ 25	$	$ 300
Husband: lunches & misc.	20		240
Wife: miscellaneous	20		240
Dry Cleaning	20		240
Animals (license, food, vet)	10		120
Beauty and Barber	20		240
Other			
Other			
Total Miscellaneous	$ 115	$ —	$ 1,380
Total Living Expenses	$1,643	$7,450	$27,166

Debt Repayment

Exhibit D, the debt repayment schedule, is the same schedule as prepared for the liability section of the net worth statement (see page 72) with the exception that the mortgage loan amount has been left out and is not included in the total. The mortgage loan payment is included in the living expenses section in Exhibit E. In some cases no payment is being made or is intended to be made and therefore it is not included in the payment schedule. For example, the loan from the parents—there is no intention on Bob and Laura's part of repaying that loan. (Parents, beware!) Additionally, the life insurance loan will not be repaid; therefore it shows no payment. Bob and Laura are paying $650 per month in debt repayment, which includes principal and interest and does not include the home mortgage. The annual amount, then, is $7,800.

Chart 7–K

Bob and Laura
CASH FLOW ANALYSIS

GROSS INCOME—from Exhibit A (page 79)		$ 34,600
LESS:		
Giving—from Exhibit B (page 80)	$2,200	
Taxes—from Exhibit C (page 80)	9,792	
Debt—from Exhibit D (page 81)	7,800	
Total Expenses		(19,792)
Net Spendable Income		$ 14,808
Living Expenses—from Exhibit E (pages 82–83)		
Housing	7,880	
Food	4,800	
Clothing	1,000	
Transportation	2,660	
Entertainment and Recreation	2,140	
Medical	1,260	
Insurance	1,536	
Children	3,360	
Gifts	1,150	
Miscellaneous	1,380	
Total Living Expenses		(27,166)
Cash Flow Margin		$(12,358)

Living Expenses

Exhibit E, the living expense schedule for Bob and Laura shows monthly living expenses of $1,643 for the 12-month period. Expenses paid other than monthly are $7,450 for a total annual living expense of $27,166.

Their mortgage payment is included under housing expenses, while the car payment is not included under transportation because it is included under the debt repayment schedule, Exhibit D. (Car payments are generally considered a more discretionary type of expense.) In every case, Bob and Laura estimated their expenses and for the monthly amounts, they estimated average expenses.

Cash Flow Margin

Bob and Laura can now summarize each of the exhibits into a cash flow analysis as illustrated on page 84. Two primary observations emerge from this summary. First of all, the cash flow margin after all living expenses are subtracted from the gross income is a negative $12,358. This means that with no further planning on their part, they will have to do one of four things: 1) increase their income, 2) reduce their expenses, 3) dip into their savings, 4) or borrow additional monies in order not to have a negative cash flow for the year.

Since Bob and Laura are typical, the chances are pretty good that they did not even know they were running a cash flow margin that was negative. It probably crept up on them month-by-month. They also probably increased their credit card debt. They may even be considering using a debt consolidation loan, or Laura may look for work outside the home. Also, it would not be unlikely for them to reduce their giving. Now that the problem has been defined, the solution is much easier to determine.

Net Spendable Income

In addition to the cash flow margin, this summary uses the concept of Net Spendable Income, which basically says that the first three priority uses of money are giving, taxes, and debt repayment. The amount of spendable income, then, is the amount left. The net spendable income concept establishes the priorities of income and says that living expenses should be the fourth priority, as opposed to typically being the first.

As I said earlier, giving should be proportionate and should come out of the first fruits (see 1 Cor. 16:2; Prov. 3:9). Taxes are an obligation to the believer and therefore a priority (see Rom. 13:7). Debt repayment is a must for the believer (see Ps. 37:21). If Scripture gives us these three priorities, then living expenses are discretionary, manageable, and, a fourth priority, biblically.

WHERE ARE YOU?

Remember that we are not yet ready to work on solutions. We are still in the process of determining where you are. Using the charts on pages 88–93 you can prepare your own cash flow summary. Some guidelines are as follows:

Exhibit A: Your Projected Income

1. The amounts should be derived from gross income before taxes and other deductions.
2. To determine monthly amounts:
   A. If you are paid on a weekly basis, use one week's pay multiplied by 4.3 (weeks per month).
   B. If you are paid every two weeks, you get 26 paychecks per year. Multiply your two-week paycheck by 2.17. This will compensate for the two months of the year in which you receive three pay checks.
   C. If the checks received are not always the same, owing to irregular hours (overtime, shift differential, etc.), use an average pay per month as the salary.
   D. If your pay is on a commission-only basis, use an average of the past few years or what you consider a reasonable income projection.
3. Dividends and interest income should be projected as annual amounts unless these funds are being received on a monthly basis.
4. Rents received should be shown as "net rents." In other words, rental income less all rental payments and expenses.
5. Include other income from all sources, such as babysitting, hobbies, crafts, gifts, etc.
6. Business income should include income from self-employment, income-producing hobbies, or other business interests.

Exhibit B: Your Giving

1. Project your giving for the year by considering each organization you support. Use the amount of pledges, a percentage of income, past giving history, or specific giving goals in your projection.

Exhibit C: Taxes

1. The best source for determining taxes is pay stubs. Use the withholdings per check and multiply by the number of pay periods per year as described for Exhibit A.
2. Tax refunds received from overpayments in the previous year should be shown as an income source.
3. If you are self-employed or have self-employment income, you will need to estimate your annual taxes.
4. Self-employment and Social Security taxes can be determined from the following chart:

Chart 7–L

SOCIAL SECURITY CHART

Year	Wage Base	Employee Rate	Maximum Payments	Self Employment Rate	Maximum Payments
1986	$42,000	7.15%	$3,003.00	12.30%	$5,166.00
1987	43,800 (est.)	7.15%	3,131.70	12.30%	5,387.40
1988	46,800 (est.)	7.51%	3,514.68	13.02%	6,093.36
1989	50,100 (est.)	7.51%	3,762.51	13.02%	6,523.02
1990	53,400 (est.)	7.65%	4,085.10	13.30%	7,102.20

Exhibit D: Debt Repayment

1. Do not forget to adjust for any debts that will be completely repaid during the year.

Exhibit E: Living Expenses

1. Many expenses, such as utilities, should be monthly averages.
2. Use estimates if you are unsure exactly what is being spent. The objective is to become as much as 80% accurate on your initial try.

3. Note that transportation expense does not include debt repayment because the auto payments are accounted for under Exhibit D.

Cash Flow Summary:

1. Note the section for listing existing cash flow margin commitments. This might include payroll deductions for retirement programs, annuities, stock purchase plans or other investments that require regular payments.
2. Funds allocated to credit unions, payroll savings plans or deposited to savings accounts are uncommitted funds since they have no specific purpose and are available for reallocation.

Chart 7–M

YOUR CASH FLOW ANALYSIS
Year: _____

GROSS INCOME—from Exhibit A $_____

LESS:

   Giving—from Exhibit B $_____
   Taxes—from Exhibit C   _____
   Debt—from Exhibit D   _____
    Total Expenses   (_____)
    Net Spendable Income $_____
     (Gross Income Less Expenses)

   Living Expenses—from Exhibit E
    Housing   _____
    Food   _____
    Clothing   _____
    Transportation   _____
    Entertainment and Recreation   _____
    Medical   _____
    Insurance   _____
    Children   _____
    Gifts   _____
    Miscellaneous   _____
     Total Living Expenses   (_____)
     Cash Flow Margin $_____
      (Net Spendable Less Living Expenses)

EXISTING MARGIN COMMITMENTS:

Company Savings Plan _____

IRA _____

Investment Commitments _____

_____ _____

_____ _____

_____ _____

Total Commitments

UNCOMMITTED MARGIN (_____)

$_____

Chart 7–N

EXHIBIT A
YOUR PROJECTED INCOME

SOURCES	Amount Received Monthly	Amount Received Other Than Monthly	Total Annual Amount
Gross Wages—Husband	$____	$____	$____
Gross Wages—Wife	____	____	____
Dividends ____	____	____	____
Dividends ____	____	____	____
Dividends ____	____	____	____
Interest ____	____	____	____
Interest ____	____	____	____
Interest ____	____	____	____
Rents ____	____	____	____
Business ____	____	____	____
Pensions and Annuities ____	____	____	____
Other ____	____	____	____
Other ____	____	____	____
Other ____	____	____	____
Total Gross Income	$____	$____	$____

Chart 7–O

EXHIBIT B
YOUR GIVING

GIVING	Organization	Monthly	Annual	Total
Church	_____	_____	_____	_____
Other	_____	_____	_____	_____
Other	_____	_____	_____	_____
Other	_____	_____	_____	_____
Other	_____	_____	_____	_____
Other	_____	_____	_____	_____
Other	_____	_____	_____	_____
Other	_____	_____	_____	_____
Other	_____	_____	_____	_____
Other	_____	_____	_____	_____
Other	_____	_____	_____	_____
Totals		_____	_____	_____

Chart 7–P

EXHIBIT C
YOUR TAX SUMMARY

DEDUCTIONS, WITHHOLDINGS AND ESTIMATES	Monthly Withholdings	Quarterly Estimates	Total Paid Annually
Federal Income Tax	$ _____	$ _____	$ _____
State and City Income Tax	_____	_____	_____
Social Security Tax	_____	_____	_____
Total Tax	$ _____	$ _____	$ _____

Chart 7–Q

EXHIBIT D
DEBT REPAYMENT

			Payment Schedule	
Creditor	Balance Due	Interest Rate	Per Month	Until When
1.				
2.				
3.				
4.				
5.				
6.				
7.				
8.				
9.				
10.				
Totals				

Chart 7–R

EXHIBIT E
LIVING EXPENSES
Year: _____

	Amount Paid Monthly	Amount Paid Other Than Monthly	Total Annual Amount
HOUSING			
Mortgage/rent			
Insurance			
Property taxes			
Electricity			
Heating			
Water			
Sanitation			
Telephone			
Cleaning			
Repairs/maintenance			
Supplies			
Other			
Total*			

EXHIBIT E (continued)

	Amount Paid Monthly	Amount Paid Other Than Monthly	Total Annual Amount
FOOD*	_____	_____	_____
CLOTHING*	_____	_____	_____
TRANSPORTATION			
Insurance	_____	_____	_____
Gas and oil	_____	_____	_____
Maintenance/repairs	_____	_____	_____
Parking	_____	_____	_____
Other	_____	_____	_____
Total*	_____	_____	_____
ENTERTAINMENT/RECREATION			
Eating Out	_____	_____	_____
Babysitters	_____	_____	_____
Magazines/newspapers	_____	_____	_____
Vacation	_____	_____	_____
Clubs and activities	_____	_____	_____
Other	_____	_____	_____
Total*	_____	_____	_____
MEDICAL EXPENSES			
Insurance	_____	_____	_____
Doctors	_____	_____	_____
Dentists	_____	_____	_____
Drugs	_____	_____	_____
Total*	_____	_____	_____
INSURANCE			
Life	_____	_____	_____
Disability	_____	_____	_____
Other	_____	_____	_____
Total*	_____	_____	_____

EXHIBIT E (continued)

	Amount Paid Monthly	Amount Paid Other Than Monthly	Total Annual Amount
CHILDREN			
School lunches	_____	_____	_____
Allowances	_____	_____	_____
Tuition	_____	_____	_____
Lessons	_____	_____	_____
Other	_____	_____	_____
Total*	_____	_____	_____
GIFTS			
Christmas	_____	_____	_____
Birthdays	_____	_____	_____
Anniversary	_____	_____	_____
Other	_____	_____	_____
Total*	_____	_____	_____
MISCELLANEOUS			
Toiletries	_____	_____	_____
Husband: misc.	_____	_____	_____
Wife: misc.	_____	_____	_____
Cleaning, Laundry	_____	_____	_____
Animal care	_____	_____	_____
Beauty, Barber	_____	_____	_____
Other	_____	_____	_____
Other	_____	_____	_____
Total*	_____	_____	_____
Total Living Expenses:	══════	══════	══════

*Transfer the totals to the cash flow analysis chart on pages 88–89.

Chart 7-S

Bob and Laura
LIFE INSURANCE

Company	Issue Date	Policy #	Type (1)	Insured	Owner	Beneficiary	Waiver of Premium	Face Value	Cash Value	Cash Value Borrowed	Yearly Premiums
PERSONAL:											
So. Trust	8-2-48	12345	W.L.	H	H	W	Yes	2,000	1,000	-0-	36
Eternal Life	8-10-66	53210	W.L.	H	H	W	Yes	25,000	2,500	2,500	400
Family Life	8-22-72	97531	W.L.	H	H	W	Yes	50,000	2,500	2,500	900
Family Life	8-22-72	97532	Term	W	W	H	Yes	50,000	—	—	200
RETIREMENT PLAN:											
BUSINESS:											
Work Company	10-20-68	?	Group Term	H	Comp.	W	Yes	10,000			
MORTGAGE:											

(1) Term, whole life, endowment, group, etc.
Do you apply dividends to reduce premium payment? _____
Are there any special features on any of the policies? (Is it paid up; guaranteed insurability rider, etc.?)

LIFE INSURANCE SUMMARY

So far we have summarized Bob and Laura's financial situation and you have completed your own cash flow analysis. You assume you are going to continue to live. However, there are two other alternatives—one is death and the other is what has been called living death or disability. In a later chapter we will look at both of these in terms of making decisions about life insurance protection and in determining how much is needed. But at this point let's see where Bob and Laura stand in the summary of their life insurance and disability insurance on page 94.

Sources and Types of Insurance

There are four sources of life insurance that Bob and Laura could have—policies that are owned personally, policies that are part of a retirement plan, policies owned by the company for which Bob works, and mortgage insurance on the home mortgage. There are also various basic types of life insurance that could be owned—whole life, endowment, term, group term, universal life, and so on.

Note that the insured can be different from the owner, who can also be different from the beneficiary.

Face Value and Cash Value

Face value is the death benefit. Cash value is the surrender value of the policy if it were to be cashed in; and cash value borrowed is the amount of money that has been borrowed on that cash value. The cash value borrowed reduces the death benefit by the amount borrowed.

Why Insurance?

In considering life insurance, there are three questions: (1) Why do you have life insurance? (2) How much life insurance do you need? (3) What kind of insurance to use?

Basically, life insurance is needed to protect the family in the event of death while net worth is being accumulated. On our financial planning diagram, life insurance could be depicted by putting an umbrella over the "Growth in Net Worth" box as illustrated on page 96. This shows the insurance needed until sufficient assets can be accumulated to provide all of the death benefit that a family needs. There may be other reasons for having insurance, such as to provide for estate liquidity, to provide for estate taxes, and maybe even to provide for charitable giving at death; but the basic reason is to provide protection.

How Much Insurance?

How much insurance is needed depends upon long-term goals and the stage of life, but basically, I recommend that families with young children have at least 10 times their annual income in life insurance plus an amount sufficient to retire any debt they have. Also, an amount needed to fund college education for young children should be included. These are obviously "rule of thumb" amounts and should be reduced over time by the amount of investment assets accumulated. The worst thing that could happen in today's environment of relatively inexpensive life insurance is to have insufficient coverage before sufficient financial resources have been accumulated to be self-insured.

Figure 7.2

THE ROLE OF INSURANCE

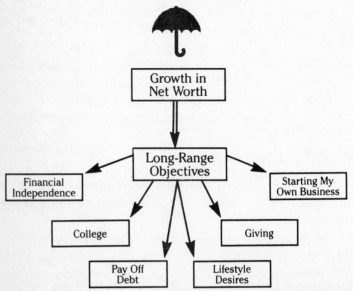

What Kind of Insurance?

The issue of what kind of insurance to have is largely an economic question revolving around two issues: "How much can you afford?" and "How long are you going to need the insurance?" If the need is temporary, then obviously term insurance, which is the least expensive, should be purchased. If the need is anticipated to be ongoing, then permanent insurance should be considered. However, permanent insurance should never be purchased when it cannot be afforded. Insurance is just that—insuring against an unexpected or unplanned for loss, and it is never anything more than that.

Many new insurance products are available, largely as a result of the impact of inflation on the insurance industry. Inflation destroyed many of the concepts of whole life life insurance, and the insurance companies responded positively by designing new insurance products. However, it has been my experience that none of these products are truly investments; they are merely forced savings plans with front-end costs. The only time that insurance makes sense from an investment standpoint is if the purchaser is in the highest of income tax brackets. The primary value, then, to permanent insurance is that it has a fixed or level premium, and that it does accumulate cash value. It is still, however, not an investment product, but an insurance product that has a *feature* of level premiums and cash value buildup. Again, life insurance should never be purchased from an investment standpoint, but only from a protection standpoint. The real issue is, "How much do I need," *not* "What kind should I buy?"

The blank form on page 98 will allow you to complete your own insurance summary and analysis.

CONCLUSION

Step 1 of the financial planning process has been completed. You have determined where you are by summarizing your present situation. By this analysis we have identified your obvious problems, financial strengths, and some action steps. However, before determining what action steps to take and which problems to focus on, you need to know what your goals and priorities are. That's the best way to head down the right path.

Chart 7–T

YOUR LIFE INSURANCE

Company	Issue Date	Policy #	Type (1)	Insured	Owner	Beneficiary	Waiver of Premium	Face Value	Cash Value	Cash Value Borrowed	Yearly Premiums
PERSONAL:											
——	——	——	——	——	——	——	——	——	——	——	——
——	——	——	——	——	——	——	——	——	——	——	——
——	——	——	——	——	——	——	——	——	——	——	——
——	——	——	——	——	——	——	——	——	——	——	——
RETIREMENT PLAN:											
——	——	——	——	——	——	——	——	——	——	——	——
——	——	——	——	——	——	——	——	——	——	——	——
BUSINESS:											
——	——	——	——	——	——	——	——	——	——	——	——
MORTGAGE:											
——	——	——	——	——	——	——	——	——	——	——	——
——	——	——	——	——	——	——	——	——	——	——	——

(1) Term, whole life, endowment, group, etc.
Do you apply dividends to reduce premium payment? _____
Are there any special features on any of the policies? (Is it paid up; guaranteed insurability rider, etc.?)

CHAPTER 8

Setting Faith Financial Goals

THE STORY OF John Goddard is very interesting. He is a man who "wanted to do it all." As a fifteen-year-old in Los Angeles, he drew up a list of everything he wanted to accomplish in his life. He had a vision of himself as a great explorer and put down such things as: explore the Nile, climb Mount Everest, retrace the travels of Marco Polo and Alexander the Great, visit every country in the world, visit the Moon. His list had a total of 127 goals.

Now nearly 60, Goddard still lives in southern California, but he has made many expeditions and is an author and lecturer. He smiles when asked about the list he made years ago.

"Nearly everyone," he says, "has goals and dreams, but not everyone acts on them. There are things on it I will never do, like climb Mount Everest or star in a Tarzan movie. Goal setting is like that. Some may be beyond your capabilities, but that doesn't mean you have to give up the whole dream."

Although Goddard believes in accomplishment, he does not feel compelled to complete every item on his list. He suggests that goals be a guideline, but not something to control one's life. Goddard also thinks that it is helpful to look at your life and ask, "If I had one more year to live, what would I do?" To date, Goddard has completed 106 of his 127 goals.

We all set goals and objectives and develop plans to achieve them. None of us ever start a vacation without knowing where we want to go; or plant a garden without knowing what we want to come up—just scattering seeds around, hoping something will come up; or build a home without giving the architect and builder any instructions—just leaving them to their own judgment. Almost anyone would say that goals are

99

important, and yet studies have shown that less than 3% of Americans have written goals.

I believe there are four vital reasons why goals should be set, and also four reasons why we don't set them. This chapter will take us from the reasons for setting goals, to the barriers to setting them, and then to the practical application of setting a faith goal.

FOUR VITAL REASONS FOR GOALS

The first and most obvious reason for setting goals is that goals provide direction and purpose. They are finish lines. Have you ever seen a sprinter start down the track and stop and look for the finish line? Of course not! Sprinters know exactly where they are headed, and all of their efforts are directed toward the accomplishment of the goal. When we set goals, our choices for activity become purposeful with more potential of being God-directed. Otherwise, circumstances, other people, feelings, etc., determine where we wind up.

Second, goals help us to crystallize our thinking. My wife and I often challenge each other with the statement, "If you aim at nothing, you will hit it every time." When you set a goal, you tend to crystallize your thinking about what you really want to accomplish. This is why I believe that goals should be written, rather than merely thought or talked about.

Third, goals provide personal motivation. When I went to Indiana University in 1960 I had an objective: it was to have a good time. I accomplished that objective, but in the process I was asked a couple of times to leave school. My grade point average hovered around the failing level. When I came back to school, met my future wife, and began to think about marriage, I also began to think about career objectives; and I set a goal to become a CPA. My grade point average went from failing to almost straight A's, and I ultimately graduated from graduate school with honors.

After college, when I was interviewing for jobs, I was often asked by the interviewers what happened. The only thing I could tell them was that I finally had a goal. I had not changed personally, but the goal toward which I was moving had changed and so provided motivation in another direction.

The fourth reason to set goals is that, by definition, a goal is a statement of God's will for me. Goals are all stated as future objectives, and only God lives in the future. So when I set a goal, I have implicitly made a statement that says, "God willing, I believe I should achieve the following . . . " Otherwise, for a Christian, a goal is a presumption.

Paul was probably one of the most goal-oriented men in the Bible. He said in Philippians 3:14: "I press toward the goal for the prize of the upward call of God in Christ Jesus." Paul knew why he was there and where he was going, and his life was governed by his goal.

Almost anyone would say that goals are important. Why, then, don't we set goals?

FOUR BARRIERS TO GOAL SETTING

Many of us don't set goals because we fear failure. If a goal is not set, there is no chance of failing to meet it. For the Christian this excuse not to set goals is ludicrous, because a Christian, in the mere act of becoming a Christian, has admitted the inability to govern his or her life. However, the fear of failure is so dominant a part of our fallen nature that it, maybe more than any other motivation, governs our behavior and is a principal reason why goals are not set.

The second reason we don't set goals is the false assumption that goal setting must take a great deal of time. A little book entitled *Tyranny of the Urgent* by Charles E. Hummel has as its thesis that we get involved in urgent but trivial matters and leave the really important things undone. We often treat goal setting like that. Even if it took a substantial amount of time, it would be worth setting aside the time. As a matter of fact, we spend much of our lives thinking about goals and objectives, but because we never write them down, we never move toward accomplishing them. The actual process of writing down goals takes only a few minutes. We are merely getting them out of our heads and onto paper.

The third reason that goals are not set is a legitimate one—we don't know what goals to set. This is especially true in the financial area because so much advice is being given, both good and bad, that we become confused. As Christians we can determine which goals to set, we can set them, and then we can develop a plan of action to achieve them. We have already looked at the financial planning diagram (see page 31) and examined the 11 goal areas—five short-term and six long-term goals.

I used to play golf in a very competitive environment with my partners and staff members in the CPA firm. On one occasion we were playing to a hole with an elevated green. We could actually "see" the hole from the fairway only by seeing the top of the flagstick indicating where the hole was. As our foursome finished the hole, one of us took the flag-stick and stuck it in the soft ground on the edge of the green near a sand trap. Well, you can imagine what happened. The following foursome, not being able to see the hole, all placed their shots to the flagstick, and ended up in the sand trap.

Like that foursome, you may have a good game plan for achieving a goal and take the right steps to achieve it, but if the goal is a wrong one, then the results can be disastrous. It is *vitally important* to know what goals to set; otherwise, activity will be channeled toward the wrong ob-jectives.

Finally, we do not set goals because many of us do not know how to set goals. We do not have a goal-setting process, and that also is a legiti-mate reason for not setting a goal.

WHAT NOT TO DO

When we learn the process of how to set goals from a faith perspec-tive, we need to look at three things *not to do*. Isaiah 43:18 says, "Do not remember the former things, / Nor consider the things of old." In setting a goal, first of all, we do not focus on the past. Focusing on the past tends to limit our thinking to our past experiences and our past failures. More importantly, focusing on the past leaves God out of the process. "Now to Him who is able to do exceedingly abundantly above all that we ask or think, according to the power that works in us" (Eph. 3:20). God is never limited by what has gone on in the past and wants to do something beyond what we can even think or imagine.

In Luke 1:18 we read the question of Zacharias to the angel in the temple: "How shall I know this? For I am an old man, and my wife is well advanced in years." Zacharias was focusing on his present resources, and that is the second thing we do *not* want to do in setting a goal. Focusing on our present resources is another way we limit God. The real question is, "What are God's resources?" Recall again Ephesians 3:20: "[God] is able to do exceedingly abundantly above all that we ask or think." What He can do is not limited by my present resources. It is only limited by His resources.

The last thing not to do in setting goals relates to those who are mar-ried. I believe that a couple should never set a goal apart from or in disagreement with one another. Most women will become widows, and if a woman has not been involved in the goal-setting process, the conse-quences can be devastating for both the woman and for the family. God puts a man and woman together to build something new, not to put two competing individuals together so that one can force goals and objectives upon the other. In the marriage relationship a couple can set goals that are unique to the couple, not to one of the individuals in the marriage. "Be of the same mind toward one another" (Rom. 12:16). The problem is that committing goals to paper in a marriage relationship requires perfect agreement, and that is threatening to many people.

SETTING YOUR FAITH GOALS

I define a faith goal as an objective toward which I believe God wants me to move. It is a question, "God, what are your plans?" or saying "God, I am available—not necessarily able, but available." Setting faith goals is a three-step process.

1. Spend Time with God

One of our critical needs in the Christian life is to spend time with our Lord in communion with Him, seeking His will and direction. God's Word clearly says that if we seek His direction and will, He will respond by giving us that direction.

> And do not be conformed to this world, but be transformed by the renewing of your mind, that you may prove what is that good and acceptable and perfect will of God (Rom. 12:2).

> Ask, and it will be given to you; seek, and you will find; knock, and it will be opened to you. For everyone who asks receives, and he who seeks finds, and to him who knocks it will be opened (Matt. 7:7–8).

Spending time with God is essential; otherwise, goal setting without God's direction becomes merely the striving after your own imagination and dreams. A faith goal is a statement of *God's will.*

2. Record the Impressions

As you spend time with God, you need to record what He seems to be saying to you. You need to take the second step, because over time, as you record the impressions you receive, assurance and conviction will result. "Now faith is the substance of things hoped for, the evidence of things not seen" (Heb. 11:1). You need to be continually asking God,

"What would You have me do?" But not, "How would You have me to do it?" As you record the answers He gives you, you become more and more sure of the goal. It is essential to have the goal recorded, because very likely there will be testing. God's objective is to build your faith, and testing does it!

3. Make the Goal Measurable

After spending time with God and recording what He seems to be saying to you, you are ready to set a faith goal. The objective toward which you believe God wants you to move must be *measurable*. For example, to be a good father is not a goal, but a purpose statement. To spend 15 minutes a day with each of my children is a goal. That can be measured. Because goals are measurable, we know definitely when they have been achieved. If you cannot determine when a goal has been achieved, then it was not a goal—it was an intention or a purpose statement.

There are several reasons to make goals measurable. First of all, a measurable goal gives a standard of accountability. If the goal is not measurable, there is no way you can be accountable for achieving it and it becomes meaningless. Second, in a husband/wife relationship, a measurable goal can only be achieved by mutual agreement. Yet one of the major problems I experience in financial counseling with couples is what I call "goal incongruity," which relates to this very issue and is, in most cases, unintentional. Goal incongruity occurs when a husband and wife have goals that are not identical. Therefore, at best, they are working to accomplish inconsistent goals; and at worst, conflicting goals.

Once you have spent time with God, recorded what He seems to be saying to you, and set a measurable objective, you have a faith goal—"an objective toward which I believe God wants me to move."

4. Take Action

Faith, in itself, is *acting* on the basis of what God wants you to do. *Faith* is an action word.

A faith goal will typically have three characteristics. The first characteristic is that its means of accomplishment may not be evident. You may not be able to see how it will happen. "By faith Noah, being divinely warned of things not yet seen, moved with godly fear, prepared an ark for the saving of his household" (Heb. 11:7). Noah had never seen rain and certainly did not know how God was going to send a universal flood, but in response to God's initiative, Noah prepared an ark. He had faith that God was going to do what He said He was going to do.

Second, a faith goal may, in many cases, be set with inadequate resources. A story similar to that of Zacharias in the temple is found in Hebrews 11:11: "By faith Sarah herself also received strength to conceive seed, and she bore a child when she was past the age, because she judged Him faithful who had promised." Setting a faith goal may mean there are "apparently" no adequate resources to accomplish that goal. If it is God's goal, it is God's responsibility to provide the resources.

Of course, you do not test God by dreaming up goals; that is why the *process* of setting the goal is so important. When you spend time with Him, you receive assurance and conviction that this is what He would have you do. Therefore, resources are of no concern. They are God's responsibility. You do not set the goal and then go to Him asking for the resources. You let Him speak to you and develop the goal, and then you trust Him for the resources.

A faith goal will typically require setting an objective without fully understanding it. "By faith Abraham obeyed when he was called to go out to the place which he would afterward receive as an inheritance. And he went out, not knowing where he was going" (Heb. 11:8). Abraham did not know where he was going, but he went in response to God's initiative. The goals that you set by faith in the financial area of your life may also need to be set without full understanding about how they will be achieved with present resources. But many of the heroes of faith in Hebrews 11 experienced the same uncertainty.

What is required on your part are two things: First, trust that God will do His part, and second, take action which is typically a first step. Abraham, Noah, Sarah, Nehemiah, Daniel, David—all exercised faith by taking a first step of action in complete dependence upon God and without full understanding, adequate resources, or seeing how their goal could be accomplished. What was required was merely the first step. God then showed the second step, and then He showed the third step, and so on.

Again, the order of the *process* is essential:

- Spend time with God.
- Record what He is saying to you.
- Set a measurable goal.
- Take the first action step.

The results of following this process are that the goal will be reached, growth will be experienced, and God will be glorified. Why? Because, first, it is God's goal and, second, He is committed to your growth as a Christian. Third, He will share His glory with no one, and it is *His* goal,

Chart 8–A

Bob and Laura
VISION FOR THE FUTURE

In five years, we see the following taking place:

GIVING:

| X | We would be giving <u>10</u>% per year.

| | We would be making additional gifts each year of: _____

| X | We would have made total gifts of: <u>$5,000 for the new chapel</u>

COLLEGE:

| X | A college fund would exist for each of our children:

Child	Type of College	Approximate Annual Cost	Total Cost
Billy	State College	$4,000	$16,000
Sue	State College	$4,000	$16,000

LIFESTYLE DESIRES:

| X | We would have made the following major purchases: (new home, car, vacations, etc.)

Item	Amount
Replace Laura's Car	$ 5,000
Redecorate Living Room	5,000
Buy a New House	20,000

| X | We would have the following type of lifestyle: (increase, decrease, or maintain present level)

<u>Maintain our present lifestyle.</u>

PAY OFF DEBT:

| X | We would have paid off the following debts:

Owed To	Total
Credit Cards	$ 1,000
Furniture	1,000
Boat Loan	5,000
Bank Loan	13,500
Parents' Loan	5,000
Auto Loan	4,000
Life Insurance	5,000

LIFESTYLE DESIRES:

We would have made the following major purchases:
(new home, car, vacations, etc.)

Item	Amount

We would have the following type of lifestyle:
(increase, decrease, or maintain present level)

and therefore He should receive the glory. *This means that God may not do it in the way that you think He should do it, or in the way that you would do it. Give God the flexibility to do things His way, with His timing and His resources.*

When I was initially developing the concepts and philosophy of biblical financial planning, I shared with my family this goal-setting process. At that time, our church was having a missions conference and our daughter, Denise, wanted to make a pledge to the missions committee. She assured my wife and me that she had gone through the process of spending time with God, recording what He had said, and felt that He would have her pledge $2 a week. As my wife and I discussed it, we realized we had a problem since our daughter only received an allowance of $1 a week. My wife and I spent an afternoon trying to determine how we were going to "help God out" and to keep Him from being embarrassed, because, obviously, Denise could not fulfill that pledge. Of course, after awhile, we realized what we were doing and stepped back to see what God would do.

Six months passed and I had forgotten about the pledge. One day my wife asked me if I realized that Denise had made her pledge of $2 every week. By the end of the year, she had literally given $104. I know that money did not come out of her savings account, because I had control of that account. Frankly, I do not know where the money came from—and it is not important. The point is that she did what she believed God would have her do—one step at a time. She did not have to see how it was going to be accomplished, and she did not have to have the resources, nor did she have to understand the process of financial planning in order to get it accomplished. At the end of the year, the pledge was fulfilled, her spiritual growth was hastened, and God received all the glory.

As adults, we face the temptation of thinking the goal is insurmountable, and we forget who it came from. My primary recommendation when setting a goal is never to set the goal "in concrete"; rather "write it in sand on the seashore," because life is a process and God is dealing with us during this process. He can give us directions more easily if we move than if we sit still, waiting for Him to write on the wall.

To determine specifically where we are going financially, look again at the financial planning diagram on page 31. In the long term, there are only six goals that can be set:

1. giving,
2. providing a college education for your children,
3. paying off debt,
4. accomplishing lifestyle desires,
5. beginning your own business, and
6. achieving financial independence.

Each of these goals, because of its financial nature, can be expressed in specific terms, and can therefore meet the criterion of being measurable.

With these six goals in mind, I have designed a Vision for the Future chart with space to answer questions under each goal-setting area. Each statement is preceded with: "In five years we see the following taking place." The chart is shown on page 106–107 with answers from Bob and Laura as an illustration.

Chart 8–B

MY VISION FOR THE FUTURE

By _____ (date), I see the following taking place:

GIVING:

☐ We would be giving _____% per year.

☐ We would be making additional gifts each year of: _____

☐ We would have made total gifts of: _____

COLLEGE:

☐ A college fund would exist for each of our children:

Child	Type of College	Approximate Annual Cost	Total Cost
_____	_____	_____	_____
_____	_____	_____	_____
_____	_____	_____	_____

LIFESTYLE DESIRES:

☐ We would have made the following major purchases: (new home, car, vacations, etc.)

Item	Amount
_____	_____
_____	_____
_____	_____
_____	_____
_____	_____

☐ We would have the following type of lifestyle: (increase, decrease, or maintain present level)

PAY OFF DEBT:

☐ We would have paid off the following debts:

Owed To	Total
_____	_____
_____	_____
_____	_____
_____	_____
_____	_____
_____	_____
_____	_____
_____	_____
_____	_____
_____	_____

BEGIN BUSINESS:

☐ We would have started our own business, which would require an investment of:

_____

_____

FINANCIAL INDEPENDENCE:

☐ We would have the following investments:

Type of Investment	Amount Invested	Annual Return
_____	_____	_____
_____	_____	_____
_____	_____	_____
_____	_____	_____
_____	_____	_____

☐ I would like to pass on to my spouse (children) the following estate:

_____

_____

_____

☐ Support my lifestyle of $_____ per month.

Use the blank chart on page 109–110 to aid you in your goal-setting process. Remember that goal setting is a prayerful process, and it is a time for discussion between husband and wife to insure congruity of goals. One way to start is for each of you, independently, to consider the goals and then discuss them together to develop a final version with joint agreement on the priorities of the goals.

If you do not have specific goals in mind, put down what comes to your mind first as you consider each of the areas shown on the chart. As you pray about these goals, God may lead you to change some or eliminate some. Be flexible and remember that this is the beginning of a process that will continue as long as you live. It cannot be completed at a point in time. Ultimately, God will reveal to you His priorities regarding your financial goals, and these priorities will be different for each individual and couple. Our financial goals are as unique as we are.

Your first priority financial goal may be to establish a college fund for your children, but there is not enough time to save an adequate amount. Your part—in other words, the action step—is to open a savings account and to adjust the budget to free up your resources for this purpose as best you can. God's part—and your area of trust—is to provide the resources.

CONCLUSION

At this point you know where you are, and you know what God would have you do financially. The next step is to begin the action steps to accomplish the goals that God has given you. Remember, you don't have to see *how*. You may not have the resources, yet you can take action without full understanding, knowing that God is in control.

- You will reach the goal.
- You will experience spiritual growth.
- You will glorify God.

CHAPTER 9

Avoiding the Most Common Financial Mistakes

NOT LONG AGO I stopped in a jewelry store to have a ring sized and was standing at the counter when I noticed a well-dressed young man purchasing a Rolex watch. A Rolex watch has become—along with a Mercedes or BMW car—a symbol of success. This man was purchasing a relatively inexpensive $2,000 Rolex, (many sell for over $10,000) and, yet, when the sales contract was written up, I noticed that it was for approximately $4,000. I thought there must have been some mistake, but it turned out that the price of the watch was $2,000, and the finance charge was an additional $2,000. This man had purchased the watch with $285 down and a balance payable of $235 per month. When he walked out of the store with that watch on, he was giving the impression that he could afford a Rolex. Yet the question is, Could he really?

Look again at the financial planning diagram on page 38. In this chapter we will focus on two of the five spending areas as we discuss Step 3 of the financial planning process, "How to Increase the Cash Flow Margin."

POSITIVE CASH FLOW

A positive cash flow margin is absolutely essential if you are to accomplish either long-term or short-term financial goals. Without a cash flow margin, you cannot accumulate in order to meet long-term goals. In addition, each of four other short-term goals—tax reduction, increased giving, debt reduction, and increased living expense—can only be met by having a positive cash flow.

In order to reduce taxes, either additional expenditures must be made for such things as increased giving, IRA's, tax sheltered investments, and the like, or income must be reduced. Either increased deductible expenses or reduced income will result in tax reduction. However, both require that there be a positive cash flow to begin the process.

Without a positive cash flow, increased giving is not an option. Once there is a positive cash flow, however, and it is used to increase giving, that decision results in decreased taxes because charitable contributions are deductible. As a financial planner, I have seen many people plan all of their tax reduction through giving. However, they had to have a cash flow margin to begin the process.

Obviously, if you want to reduce your debt principal payments, you must have the excess cash to do so. If you are "going in the hole" by overspending as was illustrated in Chapter 7, then there is no way to get out of debt until you generate a positive cash flow. After debt retirement that extra amount can be used to reduce debt further, which in turn increases the cash flow.

Lastly, if a couple or individual has as a short-term goal to increase the level of their lifestyle through a new home purchase, a new car purchase, vacations, additional gifting at Christmas, eating out more often, and so on, they must have a positive cash flow to have the additional funds.

When you look at the chart on page 114 you see that a couple earning $30,000 a year, tithing 10%, paying taxes at the rate of 18%, having no debt repayment, and spending $21,500 to live has no cash flow margin. In order to increase their living expenses by $5,000, they must increase their income by $6,800 in order to have, after tithing 10% and paying taxes of $1,100, an incremental cash flow of $5,020 with which to fund the increased living expenses.

To look at this illustration another way, if this couple were earning $36,800, tithing 10% and paying their taxes, and if they *decreased* their lifestyle by $5,000, all of that amount would go to the bottom line—the cash flow margin. Therefore, reducing living expenses causes a dollar-for-dollar increase in cash flow margin; whereas increasing living expenses requires an income increase if there is no beginning cash flow margin equal to the increase in living expenses plus the taxes and tithe paid on that amount.

This fact is often overlooked when couples plan their expenses. They forget that to fund an increase in one area through the means of increas-

Chart 9–A

	Before	After	Increase
Income	$30,000	$36,800	$ 6,800
Tithe @ 10%	(3,000)	(3,680)	(680)
Taxes @ 18%	(5,500)	(6,600)	(1,100)
Debt Repayment	–0–	–0–	–0–
Net Spendable Income	21,500	26,520	5,020
Living Expenses	(21,500)	(26,500)	(5,000)
Cash Flow Margin	$ –0–	$ 20	$ 20

ing income, they must also fund the taxes and tithe paid on that income. Couples deciding that a wife should work in order to have additional money available to spend often overlook this and find themselves going deeper into debt, first of all, by increasing their living expenses by the amount of the increased income, forgetting that the taxes must be paid on that increased income, not even to mention the additional tithe.

Living expenses and debt go hand in hand. Typically, debt is used to fund living expenses and, conversely, without the ability to borrow, the ability to increase the lifestyle is not there. Let me repeat: debt reduction and lifestyle reduction both have an immediate dollar-for-dollar impact on the cash flow margin, thereby giving the flexibility to accomplish many other goals such as tax reduction, increased giving, and accumulation.

COMMON MISTAKE #1

I have been asked many times what is the biggest financial mistake I see, and the answer is easy—*a consumptive lifestyle*. A consumptive lifestyle is simply spending more than you can afford, or spending more than you should, given your other goals and priorities. Almost everyone in America falls victim to living a consumptive lifestyle. The illustration of the man purchasing the Rolex is all too common.

Because many of my clients give substantial sums of money away, I was asked by one Christian leader what a million dollar giver looks like. My response was, "If he looks like he can give a million dollars, he probably can't." The point is that someone whose lifestyle requires substantial expenditures must earn a considerable amount of money to have enough left after taxes to fund that lifestyle. Someone in the 50% tax bracket spending $100,000 to live must earn at least $200,000 to have

$100,000 left after taxes to spend on that lifestyle. There is no way around that through tax planning, since tax planning requires that money be spent in order to reduce taxes.

We are, as a society, bombarded with a hedonistic philosophy. "Enjoy it now." "You only go around once." "Live it up." "You owe it to yourself."

Incidentally, I have observed—not at all scientifically proven, but still observed—that the more television a person watches, the higher lifestyle the person is apt to desire. Television advertising is extremely sophisticated and effective. In a similar way, the more time you spend in shopping malls, the higher lifestyle you are apt to want because you are surrounding yourself with temptation. It is much like going to the grocery store just before mealtime to do your weekly shopping. Chances are that you will spend substantially more than if you went after a meal and with a specific list in hand.

COMMON MISTAKE #2

The second most common mistake in the area of living expenses is the lack of a budget. If you have no budget, which is in effect a short-term plan, you are in reality planning to live as a responder. The best illustration of this is the person who "saves" thousands of dollars buying things on sale that are not needed. Women tend to buy responsively— hats, shoes, coats, dresses, and the like, but the problem with living as a responder is not at all a female problem. Men tend to buy, responsively—boats, cars, investments, second homes, and so forth.

The whole idea of living on a budget is distasteful to almost all of us because we view it as constraining. In fact, a budget can be one of the most financially freeing things you can have. A budget guides you and tells you when you are on course, just as a road map does when driving in an unfamiliar area. Not having the map creates fear, perhaps frustration, and certainly anxiety. The same can be said about living without a budget.

COMMON MISTAKE #3

The third most common mistake in the lifestyle area occurs in buying and selling automobiles. There may be more pride and ego involved in decisions about automobiles than any other financial decisions. A recent quote in a newspaper points this up: "Logic and automobile purchases do not go hand in hand."

Most of the time when I have the opportunity to speak to groups, I promise to tell them before I am finished the name of the cheapest car they can own. This statement always creates a lot of interest. I learned this information several years ago before I became a Christian. Although I had achieved almost every financial goal I desired, I still wanted to purchase and drive a brand new Cadillac. (This was before the Mercedes and BMW were status symbols.)

However, I was only 30 years old at the time and felt that driving a new Cadillac would be pretentious and might even be harmful for my business so I purchased an Oldsmobile 98 with all the accessories. At the time, I thought that within a couple of years, "when I was older," I would trade the car in on a new Cadillac. During that time period, however, I became a Christian and my goals and desires changed rather rapidly regarding material possessions. I lost interest in driving a new Cadillac.

As time went on, the Oldsmobile eventually had close to 150,000 miles on it—and looked it. The car had to be replaced. Once you start looking at new automobiles, your tastes change and your desires increase. I found myself looking at new cars in parking lots, on the road while I was driving, stopping at auto dealerships, and in every way lusting after a new car.

I decided at that point to do a study to determine the best car to buy from a strictly economical standpoint, taking into account all of the factors, such as gas mileage, cost of repairs, license cost, financing cost, opportunity cost of the cash paid out, insurance cost, depreciation, and the like. I spent hours and hours comparing all the numbers and coming up with a definite conclusion. I found without exception that the cheapest car I could own was the Oldsmobile! Even though the cost of repairs was substantial and the gas mileage was incredibly low, they did not offset the much higher costs related to a new car in terms of licenses, insurance, maintenance, depreciation, and financing costs, or opportunity costs. Not only was I disappointed that as a CPA I could not economically justify a different car, but I was stunned at the result. I had always assumed that the low-priced, high mileage, foreign cars would be the most economical to own.

After studying this whole issue of buying automobiles, I came to two conclusions: the cheapest car anyone can ever own is always the car *they presently own,* unless it is sold and the proceeds reinvested in a lower priced car; and the longer a car is driven, the cheaper it becomes to operate.

I did not share these results with very many people until after Febru-

Chart 9–B

CAR ANALYSIS
KEEPING OLD VERSUS BUYING NEW

	MIDPRICED AMERICAN				AVERAGE AMERICAN				EXPENSIVE FOREIGN				INEXPENSIVE FOREIGN			
	New Cash	New Fin.	3 yr	8 yr	New Cash	New Fin.	3 yr	8 yr	New Cash	New Fin.	3 yr	8 yr	New Cash	New Fin.	3 yr	8 yr
Car Cost	$15,000	$15,000	$7,500	$3,000	$10,000	$10,000	$3,500	$1,000	$25,773	$25,773	$18,000	$10,000	$5,500	$5,500	$3,100	$1,000
Gas (gallons) (1) (2)	1,500	1,500	1,500	1,500	1,350	1,350	1,350	1,350	900	900	900	900	668	668	668	668
Oil	60	60	80	100	60	60	80	100	60	60	80	100	60	60	80	100
Maintenance	—	—	300	600	—	—	300	600	—	—	300	600	—	—	300	600
Repairs	150	150	450	1,200	100	100	300	800	258	258	775	2,000	55	55	165	440
License/tax	261	261	111	24	140	140	56	15	446	446	245	70	98	98	59	17
Insurance	488	488	440	420	336	336	308	282	633	633	620	600	299	299	265	246
Principal/Int. (3)	—	4,294	—	—	—	2,862	—	—	—	7,680	—	—	—	1,574	—	—
Opportunity cost (4)	2,250	450	—	—	1,500	300	—	—	3,866	773	—	—	825	165	—	—
New car fund (5)	876	876	876	876	588	588	588	588	1,500	1,500	1,500	1,500	316	316	316	316
Depreciation	2,500	2,500	1,000	250	2,166	2,166	500	100	2,591	2,591	1,600	1,000	800	800	400	100
Annual cost	$ 8,085	$10,579	$4,757	$4,970	$ 6,240	$ 7,902	$3,482	$3,835	$10,254	$14,841	$ 6,020	$ 6,770	$3,121	$4,035	$2,253	$2,487

Assumptions:
(1) 15,000 miles/year; $1.50/gal.
(2) Gallon figures taken from *Consumer's Report*—combined city and highway
(3) Finance 80% of cost at 20% for 3 years (This figure is net of tax savings, figuring a 50% taxpayer.)
(4) Interest that could have been earned on money spent on car.
(5) Amount needed to be saved annually at 10% to buy same car in 10 years.

ary 11, 1980, when the *Wall Street Journal* published an article with an analysis of automobile ownership. The article stated that "The longer a car is kept (new or used), the cheaper it becomes to run per mile. . . . Average depreciation of a new car during the first year is 31.5% of its purchase price." The article also stated that the typical purchase price for a one-to-four-year-old used car ranges from 20% to 80% below that of a new car.

Chart 9–B on page 117 compares four different types of automobiles to illustrate the two points just made—that the least expensive car you can drive is the one you presently own, and that the longer you drive an automobile the cheaper it becomes to operate.

One of the ways, then, that living expenses can be decreased most dramatically is by merely deciding to continue driving the car you presently own. If you can also repair it and maintain it yourself, you will, over time, have substantial cash flow savings that can be invested for the future rather than be consumed in the present.

Another *Wall Street Journal* article entitled, "Riddle: Why Won't a Typical Millionaire Take You for a Ride in His Fancy Car?" appeared in May of 1985. Ed Bean reported on Thomas Stanley, a marketing professor at Georgia State University in Atlanta, who had been studying "the ways of the rich, particularly those with a net worth of at least $1,000,000, for the past 12 years." What he found, among other things, was that millionaires usually drive "four-door American sedans or Volvos with no chrome. Old station wagons are not uncommon. 'These are the most traditional people in the world,' says Mr. Stanley."

How did they become wealthy? In part by doing what we are talking about in this chapter—avoiding three of the common mistakes individuals make—having a consumptive lifestyle, not having a budget, and unnecessarily buying an automobile.

ACTION POINTS

The major key to success in reducing living expenses is recognizing that every dollar saved in the living expense category goes directly to the cash flow margin. Each living expense item must be evaluated item by item and then controlled—there is no magical way, but each reduction frees dollars for other goals.

As an illustration, look at the living expenses of Bob and Laura on pages 82–83; then examine the cuts they arbitrarily decided to make in Chart 9–C.

Chart 9–C

Bob and Laura
INCREASING YOUR MARGIN

	Monthly Amount	Annual Amount
REDUCE LIVING EXPENSES BY:		
Reduce Housing by:	$100	$1,200
Reduce Food by:	25	300
Reduce Transportation by:	50	600
Reduce Entertainment/Recreation by:	20	240
Reduce Insurance by:		786
Reduce Spending on the Children by:	90	1,080
Reduce Gifts by:		500
Reduce Miscellaneous by:	25	300
TOTAL		$5,006

Some observations regarding these decisions:

1. Some areas are not cut at all because there is no ability and/or desire to cut in that area. For example, medical expenses and clothing.
2. Many of the specific reductions come from foregoing a desired consumption or purchase, such as eliminating eating out one night per month.
3. Some items undoubtedly can be cut by merely shopping better or buying more wisely, such as in the area of insurance.
4. Many ideas for reducing expenses undoubtedly come from friends and others in similar financial circumstances.
5. Be careful not to reduce or eliminate an expense this year that would be more costly, perhaps, next year. This is especially true in the areas of maintenance and repairs on automobiles and homes.
6. James 1:5 says, "If any of you lacks wisdom, let him ask of God, who gives to all liberally and without reproach." God is pleased to give you creative ways to reduce your expenses when you come to Him humbly asking for His guidance and wisdom. It has been my experience that God gives unusual creativity to those who demonstrate a desire and obedience to His plans and purposes.

By merely choosing to do so, Bob and Laura were able to decrease their total annual living expenses by $5,006, which is an 18.4% reduction in their total living expenses. As I look at their choices, it does not appear to me that they are going to decrease their lifestyle materially by the decisions they made. However, saving $5,000 a year by consuming less will result over a long time period in an incredible amount. Remember, a dollar saved does not put a dollar into the future, but multiple dollars into the future.

THE MISTAKES OF DEBT

The common mistakes in financial planning are all, in one way or another, related to debt. Debt and lifestyle go hand in hand in American society. When you use debt to fund a consumptive lifestyle, not only do you have the consumptive lifestyle working against you financially, but you also have the additional burden of the debt working against you financially. Both should be avoided like the plague!

The Plastic Way to Debt

Avoiding the use of debt is incredibly difficult because the promotion of credit card use has made credit so easy to obtain and the temptation to use credit or debt so overwhelmingly difficult to resist. Credit card companies are spending hundreds of billions of dollars to entice each of us to spend and to use credit with cards that make spending "easier," and those amounts are a pittance when compared to the additional advertising dollars of retailers.

Using Atlanta as a test market, Sears recently introduced a new credit card called "The Discover Card." The newspaper articles at the time of its introduction reported that Sears' officials expected credit card usage to go up by 35 billion dollars as a result of the introduction of this new card. Their studies showed that the card use would be incremental borrowing rather than replacement borrowing. In other words, people would be adding to their already existing credit card debt because the new card was nothing more than an additional line of credit for them.

I was talking with a banker friend of mine one day about credit card debt and how the banking industry viewed people who paid their debt off every month. He advised me that in the banking industry, a person who uses his or her credit card for convenience sake and pays the debt off each month is known as a "deadbeat." What a difference a few years makes! When I was growing up, a deadbeat was someone who didn't pay his bills; now a deadbeat is someone who does pay his bills and does it promptly! Of course, lending institutions do not want people to pay their credit card debts each month because of the 18–21% interest that is earned on that credit card debt.

A Way Out

The *only absolute way to avoid the use of debt,* in the first place, is to have a financial plan prepared at the beginning of each year that does not allow for the use of debt, and that through self-discipline you will stick to.

The major problem most people face is how to get out of the debt that they are already in. There are only two ways to get out of debt after making the decision to avoid the use of debt: Examine the assets you have to see which ones could be sold in order to reduce debt; and in the absence of assets to sell to eliminate debt, set up a repayment schedule and strictly adhere to it.

I just recently purchased a used car from a young woman who was in the process of getting a divorce from her husband. During a test drive of the car she told me that the payments on her car, which was less than one year old, were $476 per month. This amount did not include the insurance and other ancillary costs of operation. I don't know what her annual earnings were, but $476 a month had to be a substantial portion of her monthly earnings.

She had just purchased the car less than a year ago and was now having to sell it to me for approximately two-thirds of the purchase price. In doing so, she was freeing up $476 a month or $5,712 per year in cash flow. Obviously, she will have to purchase another car, so that amount is not totally free; but she had reduced her debt by selling the assets that caused the debt.

Other assets that may be sold are investment assets, the liquidation of savings accounts, and perhaps even borrowing from the cash value of life insurance at a lower interest rate than what is being paid on credit card and consumer debt.

In determining which assets to sell in order to reduce debt, remember that the assets sold should have a lower yield or appreciation rate than the debt cost. For example, in Bob and Laura's case (see page 81), if they sell the boat in order to reduce the debt, they should be able to realize $6,000, which is the listed market value on their net worth statement, and of course this $6,000 is generating no income or appreciation. In fact, it is depreciating. They could, then, use the proceeds of that sale to eliminate the boat loan of $5,000, costing $200 per month of cash flow, and save a 14% interest rate, which is not a bad rate of return for any investment. By eliminating the boat loan through the sale of the boat, they essentially made an investment that yielded 14%.

They also could reduce their debt by selling the land, which has a market value of $5,000; they could sell one-half of their marketable securities, or they could borrow $1,000 from their life insurance cash value. In deciding whether or not to sell the real estate investment and eliminate the bank loan at 15%, they will have to determine whether the land is appreciating at a greater than 15% rate.

If they sell these assets, they will eliminate all of their monthly payments, except the home mortgage, and free up $7,800 on an annual basis, or $650 on a monthly basis, which goes to reduce the negative cash flow margin they have been facing. That $7,800 plus the $5,006 generated by reducing living expenses totals a $12,806 cash flow increase.

However, some of their income is going to disappear from the real estate investment and the securities dividends. That amount is $2,150, so the positive cash flow impact of selling assets to reduce debt is $5,650 before considering the tax ramifications of so doing.

The logical question that comes up at this point is twofold. First of all, did the selling of assets to reduce debt make economic sense? Second, what impact did it have on their tax situation?

First of all, economically they have reduced high cost debt by choosing low productive or nonproductive assets. Therefore, it has to make economic sense over time, and the impact on their cash flow is immediately a positive $5,650, and the impact on their net worth is neutral. There is no impact on the net worth because a dollar reduction in assets is offset by a dollar reduction in debt.

In Chapter 11 we will look at the tax impact of these decisions to determine whether they make tax sense. As a matter of fact, it does make tax sense. Even if it did not, the decision would still have been a good one because of the relieved pressure of not having to fund continually the negative cash flow and endure the anxiety and strain such a situation causes in a marriage.

REPAYMENT—THE HARD WAY

Not everyone has the luxury, however, of selling assets to repay debt. Many of you are perhaps deeply in debt and have no assets at all. In fact, statistically, 80% of Americans owe more than what they own; therefore, selling assets is not an option. The only option, then—other than having the spouse go to work, receiving an inheritance, or striking oil—is the slow, painful and difficult process of making monthly payments. You must decide, first of all, not to take on any more debt, and second, to set up a schedule of debt repayment.

I recommend that, rather than a debt consolidation loan, you go directly to your creditor with the schedule in hand of how you are going to repay the debt, and that you do two things:

1. Pay something on each debt each month so that the creditor knows you are serious.
2. Concentrate on eliminating the smallest debt first. You need to have some reward quickly for a difficult project. When you have eliminated the smallest debt first, then you can apply the additional amount available from not having to pay on that debt anymore, to the second smallest debt that you have. And on up the ladder, you will be building a momentum that is exciting and encouraging.

One of the other keys to repaying debt is to precommit any extra income or amounts from reduced expenses—in other words, excess cash flow—to debt repayment. This is an opportunity for you to see God work in your financial lives. He will provide funds in an unexpected and supernatural way as a result of your obedience to Him. Spiritually, what you need to be asking during this time is, "God, what would You have me learn?" not, "God, why are You treating me this way?" Chances are good that God did not force you into the debt situation, but by His mercy He will enable you to climb out of that situation.

I am often asked whether couples in a heavy debt situation should tithe or not, and I have two thoughts regarding this. First of all, tithing is no more or less spiritual than debt repayment if God owns it all. However, because God does own it all, a tithe, as a priority, is a statement of your recognition that God owns it all. In other words, I don't believe it is a yes/no question; rather it is a question relative to the individual and the circumstances. A person must, however, bear in mind the two principles: *God owns it all* and *As a priority, giving is commanded in the Bible.* The question of whether to use tithe money to fund debt repayment is a very serious spiritual decision that can only be made with much prayer and godly counsel.

Remember, faith requires a first step without full understanding and without seeing how it is all going to work out. Getting out of debt requires elements very typical of the faith walk. In most cases for the Christian it requires faith even to take the first step.

GO WITH THE GREEN

One last point on debt. Many years ago when I began thinking of financial planning as a career, I understood the importance of living on a budget. Prior to that time I used credit cards as a convenience item while I lived according to a budget. Credit cards just made record keeping easier, and because I paid the credit card statements in full each month, there was no interest cost associated with the credit cards. But then I read somewhere that the mere use of credit cards will cause a family to spend 34% more, regardless of whether the full statement is paid off each month or not. I found that totally unbelievable and spent a year trying to disprove it.

The only way to disprove the information was not to use credit cards and go on a straight cash payment system. So my wife and I put away our credit cards and lived strictly on cash. We paid cash for everything.

By using cash throughout the year, my spending mentality changed. It was much more difficult to pay $25 for a tank of gas using cash than if I used a credit card. (I still had that Olds 98, affectionately labeled "Old Blue.") Paying cash at the drugstore caused me, at the very least, to hesitate, and in most cases, to eliminate those impulsive purchases at the checkout counter. Paying cash for clothes caused me to think very seriously about the need for such items. Paying cash for car repairs caused me to examine whether it could be done less expensively, either by myself or at another place. Paying cash for airplane tickets while traveling caused me to think a second time about the trip I was taking.

The conclusion of the story is that after living on a straight cash budget for a year, without using credit cards at all, our living expenses decreased by 33% from a level I had thought was "bare bones" to begin with.

I recommend this for everyone, at least for a year, until your spending habits are adjusted and you have set a budget based upon a cash level rather than a credit card level.

You probably have some questions about this recommendation:

- Isn't there a risk in carrying cash? Of course there is. So you learn to be more cautious and plan ahead for the need for cash. I might add that the risk of overspending without planning to pay cash is greater than the loss of cash out of a purse or wallet.

- Isn't it awfully inconvenient to have cash on hand at all times? Of course it is, but the benefit of reduced spending is well worth the price paid.

- Don't I need my credit cards to establish credit? In some cases, a retailer may demand to see a credit card before cashing a check, but that is rare if you have a driver's license. This kind of situation is also a tremendous opportunity to share why you don't have credit cards and how God is faithful to provide for you in a superabundant way. Also, it may be an opportunity for you to share the gospel message. In Chapter 1, I pointed out that the Christian will be "different," not "better." We show our difference by attempting to be nonconsumptive.

- Isn't this recommendation awfully narrow-minded and restrictive? That question is answered many times. "Dishonest money dwindles away, but he who gathers money little by little makes it grow" (Prov. 13:11 NIV). Proverbs 10:4 says, "He who deals with a slack hand becomes poor, / But the hand of the diligent makes one rich." Proverbs 12:24 says, "The hand of the diligent will rule, / But the slothful will be put to forced labor." Proverbs 12:27 says, "The slothful man does not roast what he took in hunting, / But diligence is man's precious possession." Proverbs 13:18 says, "Poverty and shame will come to him who disdains correction."

Enough said!

CHAPTER 10

Designing a Personal Financial Plan

WHEN I FIRST started in the financial planning business several years ago, I really believed there was one standard financial plan. However, I was confused about the elements of a financial plan. In other words, where did investment planning fit into a financial plan? Where did tax planning fit into a financial plan? Where did estate planning fit into a financial plan? How did life insurance affect a financial plan?

I finally came to the conclusion that a financial plan is, in reality, nothing more than a projection over some time period of cash inflows and cash outflows that represent the action steps a person is taking in every area of financial planning. These action steps become a road map for the future.

Once a financial plan has been determined—in other words, the action steps determined and organized into a projection—then the financial plan can be evaluated in light of two things. First of all, does the plan improve the current situation? And second, does it help the person achieve the goals he or she actually has?

Review again the financial planning diagram on page 127. Step 1 gives a picture of where you are at the present, both from a net worth standpoint and from a cash flow standpoint. Step 2 summarizes where you would like to go—in other words, your future goals. Step 3 gives the primary action steps to achieve the long-term goals through increasing the cash flow margin. Step 4 is the way you control the financial plan. Each step is positioned on the diagram beside the area involved in that step.

Bob and Laura's cash flow decisions (Step 3 of the process) are summarized on page 128.

Figure 10.1

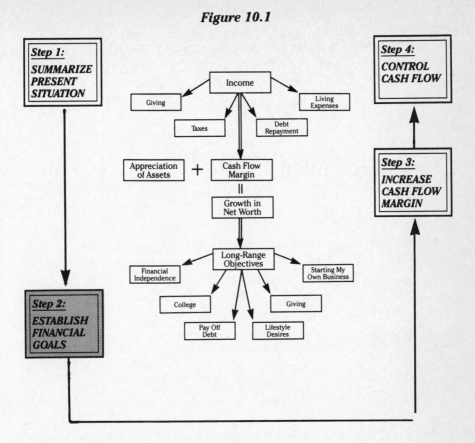

The summary of all the decisions they made is a net increase in cash flow of $13,456. It came from reducing their living expenses by $5,006, reducing their debt outflow through the sale of assets by $7,800, reducing their tax withholding by $2,500 (explained in Chapter 12), and decreasing their investment income through the sale of certain assets and increasing that income by transferring money from a savings account into a money market fund that yields a higher rate of interest.

Those action steps are then summarized into an analysis of their cash flow, both "Before Planning" and "After Planning" as depicted in Chart 10.2–B. Their financial plan is comprised of the action steps taken in the right hand column and is literally the "After Planning" summary of their cash inflows and cash outflows.

Notice that they have a net positive cash flow of $1,098 compared to a preplanning negative cash flow of $12,358. They have done nothing more than decide to go from a negative cash flow to a positive cash flow by adopting a less consumptive lifestyle and by choosing to eliminate their debt by selling assets. Now that they are generating a cash flow

Chart 10–A

Bob and Laura
INCREASING YOUR MARGIN

	Monthly Amount	Annual Amount
1. REDUCE LIVING EXPENSES BY:		
Reduce Housing by:	$100	$ 1,200
Reduce Food by:	25	300
Reduce Transportation by:	50	600
Reduce Entertainment/Recreation by:	20	240
Reduce Insurance by:		786
Reduce Spending on the Children by:	90	1,080
Reduce Gifts by:		500
Reduce Miscellaneous by:	25	300
TOTAL	310	$5,006
2. REDUCE DEBT BY:		
Sell Boat, Land, ¹/₂ Securities	——	7,800
Borrow $1,000 from insurance	——	——
Sell real estate	——	——
3. REDUCE TOTAL TAXES BY:		
Change W–4 to reduce withholding by $2,500	——	2,500
	——	——
	——	——
	——	——
	——	——
4. RESTRUCTURE TOTAL INVESTMENTS BY:		
Sell Real Estate	——	(2,000)
Put Savings in Money Market Fund ($5,000 @ 12%)	——	300
Sell Securities	——	(150)
TOTAL	——	(1850)
Total Margin Increase		$13,456

Chart 10–B

Bob and Laura
CASH FLOW ANALYSIS SUMMARY

	Before Planning	After Planning	Action Steps
INCOME:	$34,600	$32,750	Invest savings in money market fund.
LESS:			
Giving	2,200	2,200	
Taxes	9,792	7,292	Increase withholding allowances and reduce amount withheld.
Debt	7,800	–0–	Sell assets and pay off debt except mortgage.
Total priority expenses	19,792	9,492	
Net spendable income	$14,808	$23,258	
EXPENSES—LIVING:			
Housing	$ 7,880	$ 6,680	Reduce by $100/month.
Food	4,800	4,500	Reduce $25/month.
Clothing	1,000	1,000	
Transportation	2,660	2,060	Reduce $50/month by shopping for auto insurance; do maintenance at home.
Entertainment/ Recreation	2,140	1,900	Reduce $20/month.
Medical	1,260	1,260	
Insurance	1,536	750	Cancel policies with debt; replace with $100,000 term insurance.
Children	3,360	2,280	Reduce $90/month.
Gifts	1,150	650	Make some gifts; plan ahead; shop sales.
Miscellaneous	1,380	1,080	Reduce $25/month.
Total	$27,166	$22,160	Options: Increase giving;
Cash Flow Margin	($12,358)	$ 1,098	start college fund; set aside for auto.

margin, Bob and Laura can begin to accomplish their long-term goals.

In reality, their final financial plan will probably have one more element, since they must decide what to do with the positive cash flow margin of $1,098. I would suggest to them, if I were their financial planner, that they increase their giving by $1,000 to bring it up to a 10% tithe amount. That, in turn, would reduce their income taxes by something in the neighborhood of $300, giving them a net cash flow of $300 after the allocation of the margin. Their plan is certainly not a comfortable one, since there is very little margin for error. However, it is far better than the financial plan they were operating under.

The plan they now have represents the reality of their financial situation. Basically, they could not afford the lifestyle they had adopted, and they were violating a biblical principle by presuming upon the future through the acquisition of debt, probably assuming that they were going to have an increasing income with which to pay off the debt.

Now that their financial plan is in place, we will evaluate it, first of all, in light of its impact on the balance sheet, because that one summary

Chart 10–C

Bob and Laura
PERSONAL BALANCE SHEET ANALYSIS SUMMARY

ASSETS:	Before Planning	After Planning	Action Steps
Cash	$ 2,000	$ 2,000	Invest in money market fund.
Savings	5,000	5,000	
Marketable Securities	5,000	2,500	Take $2,500 and pay off debt.
Life Insurance			Borrow cash value, cancel
Cash Values	6,000	–0–	policies with loans.
Home	80,000	80,000	
Boat	6,000	–0–	Sell and pay off debt.
Land	5,000	–0–	Sell and pay off debt.
Automobile	8,000	8,000	
Furniture	5,000	5,000	
Real Estate			
Investments	15,000	–0–	Sell and pay off debt.
Total Assets	$137,000	$102,500	
LIABILITIES:			
Charge Cards	$ 1,000	–0–	
Installment Loans			
(furniture)	1,000	–0–	
Auto loans	4,000	–0–	
Debt to Relatives	5,000	–0–	
Mortgage	40,000	40,000	
Boat Loan	5,000	–0–	
Bank Loans	13,500	–0–	
Life Insurance Loan	5,000	–0–	
Total	$ 74,500	$ 40,000	
Net Worth	$ 62,500	$ 62,500	

statement measures whether a person is making progress or not. Chart 10–C on page 130 is a comparison of their balance sheet before planning and after planning.

The primary thing to notice is that their net worth did not change, even though they sold $34,500 of investments and assets in order to reduce debt. Basically, they had accumulated assets beyond their ability to accumulate. Therefore, they chose to sell the assets they could not afford in order to pay the debt. This, in turn, increased their cash flow situation to such an extent that they are now in a much stronger financial position than they were before.

The plan must also be evaluated by the second question, Does the personal financial plan move Bob and Laura toward the achievement of their long-term goals?

In light of their goals in the giving area, they have the potential to increase their giving to a 10% tithe, and they could also choose to give $5,000 for the new chapel at their church by taking the money out of their savings account. Of course, that would mean giving up the emergency fund and flexibility factor in their financial situation, but that is not to say it would not be a wise spiritual decision. The decision depends upon the prayerfully set goals that God has given them. At least, they can measure the impact of whatever financial decisions they make on their situation.

They are not making progress toward the goal of funding college education except to the extent that they can generate a positive cash flow. As they do, the funds can be allocated to this high priority goal.

A cash flow margin will also make it possible for Bob and Laura to achieve some of their major lifestyle desires such as replacing Laura's car, and they may choose to use savings account balances or checking account balances to accomplish some of these objectives. The reductions in their living expenses, especially in such areas as entertainment and gifts, may make them feel they are giving up the one goal of maintaining their present lifestyle in order to accomplish some other goals. However, that is a personal evaluation, and my evaluation is that their lifestyle will not be appreciably hurt.

One of their major objectives is to pay off debt, and all debt will be paid for under this financial plan with the exception of the home mortgage.

They also indicated they would like to have $5,000 invested in a money market fund. This is one of the action steps that they can—and should—take as a part of their financial plan. Therefore, they will accomplish this goal. In addition, they would like to pass on to their children at least $100,000. Their net worth of $62,500 is a major step toward the accomplishment of that goal and has not been reduced by the financial plan they are putting into place.

The only thing for Bob and Laura to do at this point is to take the action steps they have decided on. Until they do so, they have not exercised faith, for faith without works is dead. Faith will always require an

Chart 10–D

Bob and Laura
FINANCIAL GOAL SETTING WORKSHOP
VISION FOR THE FUTURE

In five years, we see the following taking place:

GIVING:

[X] We will be giving 10% per year.

[ ] We will be making additional gifts each year of: _____

[X] We will have made total gifts of: $5,000 for the new chapel _____

COLLEGE:

[X] A college fund will exist for each of our children:

Child	Type of College	Approximate Annual Cost	Total Cost
Billy	State College	$4,000	$16,000
Sue	State College	$4,000	$16,000

LIFESTYLE DESIRES:

[X] We will have made the following major purchases: (new home, car, vacations, etc.)

Item	Amount
Replace Laura's Car	$ 5,000
Redecorate Living Room	5,000
Buy a New House	20,000

| X | We will have the following type of lifestyle: (increase, decrease, or maintain present level) |

Maintain our present lifestyle.

PAY OFF DEBT:

| X | We will have paid off the following debts:

Owed To	Total
Credit Cards	$ 1,000
Furniture	1,000
Boat Loan	5,000
Bank Loan	13,500
Parents' Loan	5,000
Auto Loan	4,000
Life Insurance	5,000

BEGIN BUSINESS:

| | We will have started our own business, which will require an investment of:

_____

_____

FINANCIAL INDEPENDENCE:

| X | We will have the following investments:

Type of Investment	Amount Invested	Annual Return
Emergency Fund	$5,000	_____

| X | I will like to pass on to my spouse (children) the following estate:

$100,000

| | We will have adequate investment income to support our lifestyle of $_____ per month.

action step. Once the action steps have been taken and the financial plan is thus in place and working, they will need to control the living expenses—to carry out Step 4 of the financial planning process.

Again, I want to emphasize that financial planning is a process. Circumstances will change throughout the year, goals will change, and desires will change. We live in a dynamic environment and flexibility is one aspect of a financial plan. Generally, I recommend that a financial plan be reviewed at least on an annual basis and, in the earlier years of developing the discipline of financial planning, that it be reviewed and perhaps revised on a quarterly basis. As time goes on, you will find that the process of financial planning becomes almost automatic as you implement the principles and put them into practice.

Use the following pages to design your own financial plan and evaluate its impact on your balance sheet. We are now at the "perspiration point" of financial planning. However, it is also the most exciting point, because you can discover the action steps needed to achieve your real goals and to incorporate biblical principles into your daily life.

Chart 10–E

INCREASING YOUR MARGIN

	Monthly Amount	Annual Amount

1. REDUCE LIVING EXPENSES BY:
   _____   ____   ____
   _____   ____   ____
   _____   ____   ____
   _____   ____   ____
   _____   ____   ____
   _____   ____   ____
   _____   ____   ____
   _____   ____   ____
   _____   ____   ____

2. REDUCE DEBT BY:
   _____   ____   ____
   _____   ____   ____
   _____   ____   ____
   _____   ____   ____
   _____   ____   ____

3. REDUCE TAXES BY:
   _____   ____   ____
   _____   ____   ____
   _____   ____   ____
   _____   ____   ____
   _____   ____   ____

4. RESTRUCTURE INVESTMENTS BY:
   _____   ____   ____
   _____   ____   ____
   _____   ____   ____
   _____   ____   ____
   _____   ____   ____

   Total Margin Increase   ====

Chart 10–F

YOUR CASH FLOW ANALYSIS SUMMARY

	Before Planning	After Planning	Action Steps
INCOME:	_____	_____	_____
LESS:			
Giving	_____	_____	_____
Taxes	_____	_____	_____
Debt	_____	_____	_____
Net spendable income	_____	_____	_____
EXPENSES—LIVING:			
Housing	_____	_____	_____
Food	_____	_____	_____
Clothing	_____	_____	_____
Transportation	_____	_____	_____
Entertainment & Recreation	_____	_____	_____
Medical	_____	_____	_____
Insurance	_____	_____	_____
Children	_____	_____	_____
Gifts	_____	_____	_____
Miscellaneous	_____	_____	_____
Total	_____	_____	_____
Margin	_____	_____	_____

Chart 10–G

YOUR PERSONAL BALANCE SHEET ANALYSIS SUMMARY

ASSETS	Before Planning	After Planning	Action Steps
Total Assets			

LIABILITIES

	Before Planning	After Planning	Action Steps
Total Liabilities			
Net Worth			

11

Control the Flow

MANY PEOPLE TELL me stories about the cookie jar where Grandpa and Grandma used to keep all of their cash. As income was earned, it went into the cookie jar. As needs arose, the money to pay for them was taken out of the cookie jar. When the cookie jar was empty, there was no more spending until more cash was received.

As time went on and the management of expenses became more complex for our grandparents, they gave up the cookie jar and started to use an envelope system. Money was placed in various envelopes according to the allocations of the income—one envelope for food, one envelope for clothes, one envelope for giving, one envelope for insurance, and the like, depending on how many allocations they wanted to have. But the cookie jar principles still applied. The income was allocated and placed into the envelopes, and money was spent in the various areas allotted. When an envelope was empty, the spending stopped until more cash was received and placed in it.

In examining the cookie jar or envelope system, we find *three basic principles* that were applied in order to control cash flow. The first principle is that money was always preallocated. In the era of the cookie jar, the inflow and the outgo were so closely related that it was not necessary to allocate to various categories. The spending was done as the need arose. However, as both income and kinds of expenses increased, the income needed to be preallocated and placed in an envelope for the intended use.

The second principle is that spending always stopped when the envelope or cookie jar was empty. The reason was simple—there were no alternatives.

Figure 11.1

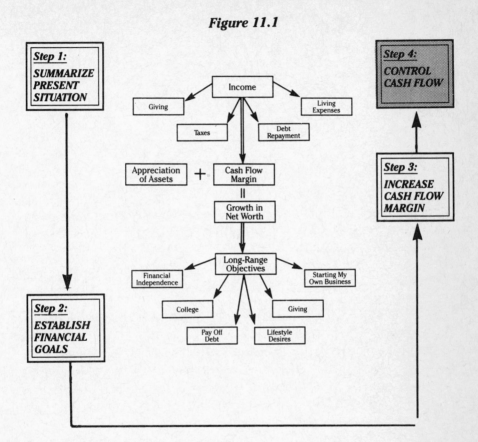

A third principle is that the individuals always had a current awareness of the financial situation relative to the planned situation. It was very simple to determine whether there was any money left in the envelope or the cookie jar. If there was, not all of the spending had been done that the plan called for. If, on the other hand, it was empty, the plan had been accomplished.

The same guiding principles need to be evident in any cash flow control system: A preallocation of income, an end to spending when the spending limit is reached, and a current awareness of the financial situation relative to the plan.

CASH CONTROL PROCESS

In order to put a cash control system in place, you must accomplish five steps. I want to caution you that this five-step process may take as much as two years to accomplish, and *it is essential that there be flexibility*. A budget—and I have avoided using that word as much as possible, but that is in effect what we are discussing—is never the law, but rather a guide.

The process is as follows:

STEP 1: ESTIMATE YOUR LIVING EXPENSES

Using the charts on pages 91–93, estimate your living expenses in as much detail as possible. I suggest that you not attempt to estimate them down to the penny, but rather shoot for 80% accuracy this first time through.

STEP 2: RECORD WHAT ACTUALLY HAPPENS

At this point in the process, you are capturing the data in order to evaluate how closely your actual expenses are to what you estimated them to be. (Recording the data and increasing your awareness also help you control your spending.) You will need a system of summarizing all of your expenses according to the expense categories you previously estimated. You can do this on worksheets or even on your computer with a compatible software program. (This may be the time you have been looking for to justify that personal computer expense!)

STEP 3: ESTABLISH A BUDGET

After you have estimated your expenses and recorded what has actually happened over a time period of three to twelve months, it is time to establish a budget. Perhaps you will want to use the percentage guide in Chart 11–A on page 141 for setting up your own budget.

STEP 4: CONTROL THE BUDGET

Almost any system can be used. Many couples I know still use the basic envelope system to control their budget. They put a preallocated

Chart 11–A

ESTIMATE YOUR EXPENSES
PERCENTAGE GUIDE FOR FAMILY INCOME

	$20,000	$30,000	$40,000	$50,000	$60,000	$	%
Gross Income	$20,000	$30,000	$40,000	$50,000	$60,000	—	—
Giving	10%	10%	10%	10%	10%	—	—
Taxes and Social Security	17%	18%	19%	22%	22%	—	—
Net Spendable	$14,700	$21,500	$28,300	$33,700	$40,400	—	—
Housing	35%	35%	30%	29%	26%	—	—
Food	20%	16%	13%	11%	10%	—	—
Clothing	5%	5%	5%	4%	4%	—	—
Transportation	13%	10%	9%	8%	7%	—	—
Entertainment/ Recreation	6%	7%	7%	8%	8%	—	—
Medical	3%	3%	3%	3%	3%	—	—
Insurance	2%	3%	3%	3%	3%	—	—
Children	3%	2%	2%	2%	2%	—	—
Gifts	2%	2%	2%	2%	2%	—	—
Miscellaneous	5%	5%	5%	5%	5%	—	—
Margin	5%	12%	21%	25%	30%	—	—

ASSUMPTIONS:
1. Figures are based on a family of four.
2. The tax deductions are giving, interest on home mortgage, and state, sales and property taxes (average).
3. Home is owned.
4. There is no debt other than home mortgage.
5. All social security withholdings are from one wage earner.
6. The estimates are based on 1985 tax schedules and allowable deductions.
7. All living expenses are percentages of net spendable income.
8. Margin can be used for other expenses (debt, private education, savings, etc.)

amount of money each month into various envelopes and stop spending when the envelope is empty.

Another alternative is a sheet of paper for each preallocated spending category. List on the sheet of paper the date, the purpose, the deposit, the withdrawal, and the balance for that expense category just as you would in a checkbook ledger.

A more sophisticated system that I recommend for many of my clients is one that uses checkbook-type ledgers in place of the envelopes. I recommend this system because we are accustomed to using checkbooks and recording checks as they are written, and because the checkbook ledger serves in the same way as the envelope.

An overview of the cash control system using checkbook ledgers is depicted in Figure 11.2.

Using the Cash Control System

Refer to the example situation in Chart 11–B, and Figures 11.4 and 11.5 as you read the points below.

- The living expense page in Chart 11–B reflects the action steps taken to increase margin.
- Accountability areas have been selected. *H* marks those monthly expenses the husband will be accountable for and *W* marks those monthly expenses the wife will be accountable for.
- The monthly accountability areas have been totaled. These are the amounts that will be transferred to husband and wife during the month.
- A paycheck or income from any source is deposited into the checking account. An entry reflecting this is made in the Deposits and Allocations Ledger. The example assumes a semi-monthly pay period; checks on the 1st and the 15th, or 24 checks per year. Regardless of the pay periods, it will be necessary to fund the husband ($610) and the wife ($690) each month to meet the household expenses.
- If you are paid weekly or bi-weekly (every 2 weeks or 26 checks per year), then you may run short at a given point in the year on some "annual ledger" deposits. However, you will get extra checks two times per year on a bi-weekly pay period or four times per year if on a weekly pay period. These extra checks should make up the shorted amounts by the end of the year.

Figure 11.2

CASH CONTROL OVERVIEW

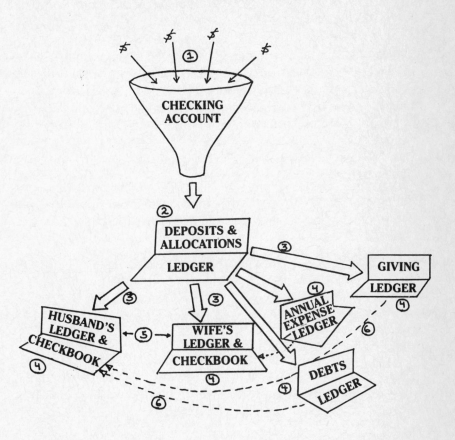

1. All funds are deposited in one checking account.
2. Each deposit is noted in the deposits and allocations ledger.
3. At specific pay intervals, each major ledger is given a deposit according to the allocation. schedule. The allocation is noted as a withdrawal from the deposits and allocations ledger.
4. Allocations are noted as deposits in each ledger.
5. Cash is disbursed through the husband's and wife's checkbooks and ledgers. Their spending must be limited to the allocated amounts.
6. As annual expenses (or giving or debt payments) are made, a transfer is made from the annual expense ledger to the husband's or wife's ledger and checkbook. The check is then written for the expense.
7. The projected annual cash flow margin should be accounted for in the checking account at the end of the year.

- Transfers are made from the Deposits and Allocations Ledger to the ledgers for husband, wife, giving, and annual expense. This has the effect of dividing money into "envelopes." The amount allocated establishes the level of spending. The annual and giving allocations are annual amounts divided by 24 (assuming two checks per month).

- The annual expense ledger is used for those expenses not paid on a regular basis. For example, automobile insurance may be paid on a quarterly or twice yearly basis. In this case, the monthly increment of auto insurance would be allocated to the annual expense ledger. The allocation should be the total annual expenses from the living expense form (Chart 11–B) divided by the number of paychecks per year.

- Husband and wife write checks for expenses in their accountability areas.

  NOTE: If there is a debt situation, then allocations will have to be made to a debt ledger and accountability for debt payment assigned.

- Transfers are made from the giving and annual expense ledgers to meet payments that are not a part of monthly income and expenses.

  NOTE: Transfers from nonmonthly expense ledgers are made to husband and wife ledgers prior to checks being written primarily to simplify balancing the checkbook. It is just as acceptable to note the giving or annual expense ledger as though they were checkbooks and checks were written directly from them.

- How much is left to spend? Look in the "envelope"; that is, check the bottom line.

Chart 11–B

(1)

LIVING EXPENSES
Year: _____

	Amount Paid Monthly	Amount Paid Other Than Monthly	Total Annual Amount
HOUSING			
Mortgage/rent	290		3480
Insurance		280	280
Property taxes		1000	1000
Electricity	55		660
Heating	35		420
Water	25		300
Sanitation			
Telephone	35		420
Cleaning			
Repairs/maintenance	5		60
Supplies	5		60
Other			
Total* (H)	450	1280	6680
FOOD* (2.)→(W)	375		4500
CLOTHING*		1000	1000
TRANSPORTATION			
Insurance		320	320
Gas and oil H 85 W 45	130		1560
Maintenance/repairs		180	180
Parking			
Other			
Total*	130	500	2060
ENTERTAINMENT/RECREATION			
Eating Out (H)	40		480
Babysitters (W)	10		120
Magazines/newspapers (H)	15		180
Vacation		820	820
Clubs and activities		300	300
Other			
Total*	65	1120	1900
MEDICAL EXPENSES			
Insurance (W)	60		720
Doctors	20		240
Dentists	20		240
Drugs	5		60
Other			
Total*	105		1260

LIVING EXPENSES (continued)

	Amount Paid Monthly	Amount Paid Other Than Monthly	Total Annual Amount
INSURANCE			
Life	_____	750	750
Disability	_____	_____	_____
Other	_____	_____	_____
Total*	_____	750	750
CHILDREN			
School lunches	30	_____	360
Allowances	20	_____	240
Tuition (W)	_____	1560	1560
Lessons	_____	_____	_____
Other	10	_____	120
Total*	60	1560	2280
GIFTS			
Christmas	_____	225	225
Birthdays	_____	75	75
Anniversary	_____	50	50
Other (W)	25	_____	300
Total*	25	350	650
MISCELLANEOUS			
Toiletries (W)	20	_____	240
Husband: misc. (H)	20	_____	240
Wife: misc. (W)	20	_____	240
Cleaning, Laundry (W)	15	_____	180
Animal care (W)	10	_____	120
Beauty, Barber (W)	5	_____	60
Other	_____	_____	_____
Other (3) (H) = $610 (W) = $690	90	_____	1080
Total*			
Total Living Expenses:	1300	6560	22160

*Transfer the totals to the cash flow analysis chart on page 136.

Figure 11.3

DEPOSITS AND ALLOCATIONS LEDGER

RECORD ALL CHARGES OR CREDITS THAT AFFECT YOUR ACCOUNT

NUMBER	DATE	DESCRIPTION OF TRANSACTION	PAYMENT/DEBIT (-)	√ T	FEE IF ANY (-)	DEPOSIT/CREDIT (+)	BALANCE 750	00
④	8/15	Deposit Paycheck				946 00	1696	00
	8/16	Transfers To:						
		Husband	305 00					
⑤		Wife	345 00					
		Giving	125 00					
		Annual	273 00				648	00
	8/20	Dividend From ABC Co				150 00	798	00
	8/25	Sold Old Lawnmower				75 00	873	00

Figure 11.4

HUSBAND'S CHECKBOOK AND LEDGER

RECORD ALL CHARGES OR CREDITS THAT AFFECT YOUR ACCOUNT

NUMBER	DATE	DESCRIPTION OF TRANSACTION	PAYMENT/DEBIT (-)	√ T	FEE IF ANY (-)	DEPOSIT/CREDIT (+)	BALANCE 10	00
⑤	8/16	Transfer From Deposits				305 00	315	00
	8/16	Gas Co.	25 00				290	00
⑥	8/16	Electric Co.	31 00				259	00
	8/16	Cash (For Gas & Misc)	20 00				239	00
⑦	8/16	Transfer From Giving				105 00	344	00
	8/16	First Baptist Church	105 00				239	00
	8/20	Transfer From Giving				25 00	264	00
	8/20	Campus Crusade	25 00				239	00	⑧
	8/23	VISA-Debit (For Gas)	15 00				224	00

Figure 11.5

WIFE'S CHECKBOOK AND LEDGER

RECORD ALL CHARGES OR CREDITS THAT AFFECT YOUR ACCOUNT

NUMBER	DATE	DESCRIPTION OF TRANSACTION	PAYMENT/DEBIT (-)	√ T	FEE IF ANY (-)	DEPOSIT/CREDIT (+)	BALANCE 25	00
⑤	8/16	Transfer From Deposits				345 00	370	00
	8/16	Cash For Groceries	100 00				270	00
⑥	8/18	Dr. Jones	25 00				245	00
	8/20	Joe's Service Station	20 00				225	00
⑦	8/25	Transfer From Annual				15 00	240	00
	8/25	Rich's (Jim's Birthday)	15 00				225	00	⑧

Figure 11.6

GIVING LEDGER

RECORD ALL CHARGES OR CREDITS THAT AFFECT YOUR ACCOUNT

NUMBER	DATE	DESCRIPTION OF TRANSACTION	PAYMENT/DEBIT (-)	√ T	FEE (IF ANY) (-)	DEPOSIT/CREDIT (+)	BALANCE
							5 00
⑤	8/16	TRANSFER FROM DEPOSITS				125 00	130 00
	8/16	TRANSFER TO HUSBAND (FOR F.B.C.)	105 00				25 00
	8/20	TRANSFER TO HUSBAND (FOR CAMPUS CRUSADE)	25 00				0 0 ⑧

Figure 11.7

ANNUAL EXPENSE LEDGER

RECORD ALL CHARGES OR CREDITS THAT AFFECT YOUR ACCOUNT

NUMBER	DATE	DESCRIPTION OF TRANSACTION	PAYMENT/DEBIT (-)	√ T	FEE (IF ANY) (-)	DEPOSIT/CREDIT (+)	BALANCE
							125 00
⑤	8/16	TRANSFER FROM DEPOSITS				278 00	403 00
	8/25	TRANSFER TO WIFE (GIFT)	15 00				388 00 ⑧

Figure 11.8

RECORD ALL CHARGES OR CREDITS THAT AFFECT YOUR ACCOUNT

NUMBER	DATE	DESCRIPTION OF TRANSACTION	PAYMENT/DEBIT (-)	√ T	FEE (IF ANY) (-)	DEPOSIT/CREDIT (+)	BALANCE

Incorporating Principles into Your Budget

The cash control system also allows the incorporation of several important basic principles.

Assigned accountability. Husband and wife each have areas of budget responsibility. For example, the husband may be responsible for mortgage and utility payments while the wife is responsible for food and miscellaneous spending. Each is assigned the cash allocations necessary to fulfill these functions.

Immediate feedback on how actual spending measures against planned spending. The key is to know as soon as possible when budget limits have been reached.

Consistent discipline. Is a budget extra work? You bet it is. However, once the budget is established, it should not require more than 20 to 30 minutes over an entire week, and the benefits are more than worth the effort. (Eventually it will require 20–30 minutes a month.)

Strict limitation of credit card use. Nothing will destroy a budget faster than having to meet unexpected debt payments. Use credit cards only as a check (a debit card) that requires a prompt accounting within the budget.

Regular accumulation of all cash flow margin. All funds not used during the month are transferred to savings so that each portion of the budget has a zero balance at the end of the month. If spending is done on an average basis, then it will be necessary during some months to transfer from savings back into the budget.

Flexibility. At times it may be necessary to use funds allocated for one purpose for some other purpose. This can be done but it requires a specific decision each time a transfer is made. For example, you may decide to give up entertainment money to buy clothes. The budget allows you to do this in a visible manner.

Questions and Answers on Cash Control

1. **Question:** Clothing expense is lumped in with annual expenses. Can I consider this and other items separately?

   Answer: You can have all the detail you want. There are several ways to do this. You can set up a separate ledger for clothing. This is probably the simplest way. Or you can subdivide any ledger into components. For example, the annual expense allocation ledger could be divided into clothing, vacation, gifts, auto repair, insurance, taxes, and the like. You can use page markers such as paper clips within a ledger book to separate the different areas, or you can color code the edges of the pages.

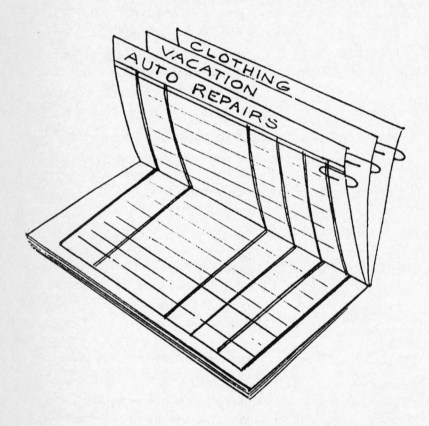

You will have to determine how much of annual expenses would be allocated to each area and simply make transfers back to husband and wife or individual checkbooks as before.

A monthly allocation for clothing could also be made directly to the husband's or wife's checkbook ledger.

2. **Question:** How do I find the cash balance of my checking account?

Answer: Add the bottom figure of each of the ledgers together:

Deposits Ledger Balance
+ Husband's Ledger Balance
+ Wife's Ledger Balance
+ Giving Ledger Balance
+ Annual Expenses Ledger Balance
= Balance in the checking account

(After correcting for checks and deposits
not shown on the bank statement)

3. **Question:** Where do I put checking account service charges?

   Answer: Subtract all bank statement service charges from the Deposits and Allocations Ledger.

4. **Question:** How many ledgers can I have?

   Answer: All you want. But remember, the more ledgers you have, the more cumbersome the system becomes. You may want to start with several to make sure you have control of each area of spending. As you become familiar with how the system works, and disciplined to living within your allocations, you may want to simplify by combining several ledgers into one.
   The overall admonition is: KEEP IT SIMPLE.

5. **Question:** How do I balance my checkbook with all these ledgers and both husband and wife writing checks?

   Answer: It is really no different than balancing with one checkbook except that the balances in the different ledgers must be considered. Deposits on the bank statement have to be reconciled with the Deposits and Allocations Ledger. Each canceled check has to be reconciled with the husband's or wife's checkbook just as you normally do with one checkbook.

6. **Question:** What if I use a credit card for a purchase?

   Answer: Transfer funds from the appropriate ledger into the debt ledger. Then when the bill arrives the funds will be available to pay it and avoid interest charges. If the funds are not available to transfer to the debt ledger, then the use of credit cards is wrong.

7. **Question:** What if I make a purchase with a debit card?

Answer: Although a debit card is used just as a credit card is used, the transaction is treated the same as writing a check. Instead of being billed for the purchase, the purchase amount will be deducted from your checking account. Since it is the same as a check, an entry for this amount should be made in your check ledger as soon as possible. A debit card is a good cash control tool and is recommended over the credit card. VISA and MasterCard banks can supply debit cards.

8. **Question:** Can I use my margin for special purchases?

Answer: You can use the margin for any purpose you desire— **but** remember that the reason for generating margin is to meet long-range goals and priorities. If you use the margin today, you give up the opportunity to meet long-range goals tomorrow.

9. **Question:** I am paid on a commission-only basis so my income is variable. How do I handle this?

Answer: Keep in mind that only a fixed amount of money is allocated to living expenses each month. All funds are deposited into the checking account and accounted for in the Deposits and Allocations Ledger. In high commission periods a surplus should develop, which should supply funds during low (or no) commission periods. Obviously the best way to start the budget is during a high (income greater than expenses) period. If this is not possible, then it may be necessary to delay allocating funds to annual expenses and concentrate on allocating only for present living expenses until commissions improve.

10. **Question:** I am self-employed. Will the budget work for me?

Answer: It works the same as for employed people and those with variable incomes. You may need an additional ledger to account for self-employment taxes and for federal and state withholding taxes. Each time a deposit is made, then the transfer of an appropriate percentage for taxes should be made to a tax ledger. This is an untouchable ledger; that is, this money is not available for transfer for any other purposes. If you do not have the discipline not to spend tax money, then open a separate savings account to hold these funds.

11. **Question:** I like to keep some cash when I deposit my paycheck. How do I account for this in the budget?

    Answer: What is the cash for? That is the chief issue. If you keep cash, then simply account for it by reducing the amount transferred from the Deposits and Allocations Ledger to the appropriate ledger. For example, the husband keeps $50 for gasoline and miscellaneous cash. Then he would reduce the amount that is allocated to his checkbook by $50.

12. **Question:** I have some annual expenses coming due but do not have the cash available to meet them and the needed household expenses. How can I start the budget?

    Answer: The ideal way to start a budget is to have a lump sum of money available for annual expenses. If we start the budget with $2,000 available, during the year we would dip into the $2,000. By the end of the year we would have recovered through regular annual expense allocations and still have $2,000.

    If you do not have the initial cash, then every time an annual expense comes due, you will have to decide what you are going to give up in order to meet that expense. However, if you keep making annual allocations on a regular basis, you will eventually overcome this problem.

13. **Question:** I did not see any place in the budget for furniture, home furnishings, improvements or appliance replacement. Where are these covered?

    Answer: These are major items and their purchase is made as a discretionary use of margin.

Establish Your Cash Control System

With this system of cash control clearly in mind, you can follow the steps below and use the Living Expense form on page 155–156 to set up your own cash control system.

- Update the Living Expense form to reflect any changes from the adjustments made to increase your margins.
- Determine the areas of accountability for husband *(H)* and wife *(W)*.
- Decide how many ledgers (expense categories) you want to use. You need at least three:
  1. Deposits and allocations
  2. Husband's expenses
  3. Wife's expenses
  You may want to add:
  4. Annual expenses
  5. Giving
  6. Debts
  7. Taxes (if you are self-employed)
- Implement the budget.

STEP 5: EVALUATE AND REVISE

By now you may have forgotten where we were in the process of setting up a cash flow control system, but the final step should not be overlooked. Once you have been operating on a budget (the system described or your own), you need to evaluate and revise the budget periodically. This should be done at least on an annual basis, but more frequent revisions may be required as you are beginning. In my own experience, I have found that it does not take more than about two or three hours per year to set up a new budget and, on a monthly basis, 20 to 30 minutes to determine where I am relative to my financial plan. It's an exciting time. It tells me a lot about how I am doing as a steward of God's resources.

Chart 11–C

LIVING EXPENSES
Year: _____

	Amount Paid Monthly	Amount Paid Other Than Monthly	Total Annual Amount
HOUSING			
Mortgage/rent	_____	_____	_____
Insurance	_____	_____	_____
Property taxes	_____	_____	_____
Electricity	_____	_____	_____
Heating	_____	_____	_____
Water	_____	_____	_____
Sanitation	_____	_____	_____
Telephone	_____	_____	_____
Cleaning	_____	_____	_____
Repairs/maintenance	_____	_____	_____
Supplies	_____	_____	_____
Other	_____	_____	_____
Total*	_____	_____	_____
FOOD*	_____	_____	_____
CLOTHING*	_____	_____	_____
TRANSPORTATION			
Insurance	_____	_____	_____
Gas and oil	_____	_____	_____
Maintenance/repairs	_____	_____	_____
Parking	_____	_____	_____
Other	_____	_____	_____
Total*	_____	_____	_____
ENTERTAINMENT/RECREATION			
Eating Out	_____	_____	_____
Babysitters	_____	_____	_____
Magazines/newspapers	_____	_____	_____
Vacation	_____	_____	_____
Clubs and activities	_____	_____	_____
Other	_____	_____	_____
Total*	_____	_____	_____
MEDICAL EXPENSES			
Insurance	_____	_____	_____
Doctors	_____	_____	_____
Dentists	_____	_____	_____
Drugs	_____	_____	_____
Other	_____	_____	_____
Total*	_____	_____	_____

LIVING EXPENSES (continued)

	Amount Paid Monthly	Amount Paid Other Than Monthly	Total Annual Amount
INSURANCE			
Life	_____	_____	_____
Disability	_____	_____	_____
Other	_____	_____	_____
Total*	_____	_____	_____
CHILDREN			
School lunches	_____	_____	_____
Allowances	_____	_____	_____
Tuition	_____	_____	_____
Lessons	_____	_____	_____
Other	_____	_____	_____
Total*	_____	_____	_____
GIFTS			
Christmas	_____	_____	_____
Birthdays	_____	_____	_____
Anniversary	_____	_____	_____
Other	_____	_____	_____
Total*	_____	_____	_____
MISCELLANEOUS			
Toiletries	_____	_____	_____
Husband: misc.	_____	_____	_____
Wife: misc.	_____	_____	_____
Cleaning, Laundry	_____	_____	_____
Animal care	_____	_____	_____
Beauty, Barber	_____	_____	_____
Other	_____	_____	_____
Other	_____	_____	_____
Total*	_____	_____	_____
Total Living Expenses:	_____	_____	_____

*Transfer the totals to the cash flow analysis chart on page 136.

CHAPTER 12

Tax Planning

IF THERE IS one cash outflow that everyone is anxious to reduce, it is income taxes.

Some time ago I had a client in my office who charged me to help him plan to pay zero taxes. He was a professional who earned a very good income, and yet he was adamant that he did not want to pay taxes. He did not agree with the way the government spent his money. I was tempted to ask him whether he would like to give up his automobile—because the road system would not be maintained without taxes—or whether he could sleep at night with no military forces to protect him, and whether he would like not to have national parks to visit, and so on.

I am in no way proposing that we should pay more than we rightfully owe in taxes. There is a big difference, however, between *tax avoidance* and *tax evasion*. Tax evasion results in a jail sentence; tax avoidance results in lower taxes, but almost never does it result in *no* taxes. Tax avoidance is planning wisely and prudently to pay a *fair share* of taxes, but no more than what is rightfully owed.

I have often reflected on our attitude toward taxes and asked myself the question, Why is it that we detest paying taxes? I believe the answer is multifaceted, but the primary reason is that we get no perceived benefit from paying taxes. Only in this area of our finances do we feel that once the money is gone, it seems to be gone forever. For the salaried and those living on a fixed income, taxes take a disproportionate share of income compared to those who have the opportunity and ability to use various tax planning tools and techniques.

When I was a practicing CPA, I prepared hundreds of tax returns each year, and was asked hundreds of times over the course of several years, "How can I reduce my taxes?" I had a facetious answer for that question:

157

"It's easy to reduce your taxes—just reduce your income." It's a guaranteed way to reduce taxes, and there is no risk to it. The point is that if your taxes are going up, your income is also going up. Taxes need to be put into proper perspective, and the proper perspective is that income taxes are levied only when there is income earned.

The second guaranteed way to reduce taxes is to spend more money on deductible items, such as charitable contributions, medical bills, interest costs, professional fees and the like. As I pointed out in an earlier chapter, there is no such thing as a free tax deduction. If you are in the 15% tax bracket, then a dollar spent on a deductible item costs you eighty-five cents cash out of pocket. True, it reduces your taxes, but there has been a cost to it. I can state unequivocally that there is no free tax deduction anywhere, at any time, for anything! When you read or hear of persons who pay no taxes or who pay low taxes and have huge incomes, that may be true in the short term because of their high deductions, but those deductions have to be paid for at some time. Here is the guiding principle for tax deductions:

> *Don't ever expect to get a free tax deduction and* **never** *make a financial decision on the basis of its tax deductibility.*

It is easy for a tax accountant to make the client happy by having him overpay on withholdings and quarterly tax estimates during the year so that he always gets a refund. I don't believe this is ethical, and it certainly does not make good economic sense. My general rule for this area is:

> *Getting a refund check is a sign of poor stewardship.*

A refund check means that the tax payer has planned poorly. The United States government does not require anyone to pay in tax withholding or quarterly estimates any more than what the taxpayer has determined the actual liability will be. A refund check is, in almost every case, a sign of poor planning.

I know that the two preceding general principles may be difficult to deal with personally, because they go against the grain of everything you thought, and perhaps even the way you have planned. For example, many people plan to have that refund check in order to make major purchases each year, but what they are really doing is admitting they do not have the discipline to save for that major purchase. Please remember that tax planning does not have to be a mystery or even very difficult, especially if you understand the above two principles.

SCRIPTURAL INSIGHTS ON TAXES

I have been looking in the Bible for the verse that says, "Thou shalt not pay any taxes." Unfortunately, I haven't been able to find it; nor have I been able to find a verse that tells me exactly how much I should pay in income taxes. However, I do find many principles throughout Scripture that directly apply to income taxes.

- "Dishonest money dwindles away, but he who gathers money little by little makes it grow" (Prov. 13:11 NIV).
- "He who is faithful in what is least is faithful also in much; and he who is unjust in what is least is unjust also in much" (Luke 16:10).
- "But we have renounced the hidden things of shame, not walking in *craftiness* nor handling the word of God deceitfully, but by manifestation of the *truth* commending ourselves to every man's conscience in the sight of God" (2 Cor. 4:2, italics mine).
- "Render therefore to all their due: taxes to whom taxes are due, customs to whom customs, fear to whom fear, honor to whom honor" (Rom. 13:7).
- "Is it lawful for us to pay taxes to Caesar or not? . . . 'Show Me a denarius. Whose image and inscription does it have?' They answered and said, 'Caesar's.' And He said to them, 'Render therefore to Caesar the things that are Caesar's, and to God the things that are God's' " (Luke 20:22, 24, 25).
- "Let your light so shine before men, that they may see your good works and glorify your Father in heaven" (Matt. 5:16).
- "Without counsel, plans go awry, / But in the multitude of counselors they are established" (Prov. 15:22).

Let me summarize these verses for you:

- You are called to be salt and light to a dying world. One of the ways that you are salt and light is by your good stewardship, which *may* require paying taxes.

- Your choice is fraud or faithfulness. You may reduce taxes by illegal or questionable means, but faithfulness requires you to use good planning and honesty to reduce taxes. Your objective is faithfulness—not tax reduction.
- Some taxes are certainly due, because our government has supplied services. Quite frankly, the freedoms and protection we enjoy in the United States are unparalleled anywhere in the world, and I believe that we all have a part in paying for these privileges. (I am not endorsing wastefulness and poor decisions on the part of our government, but the way to change that is through changing our representation in Congress.)
- Be a planner—not a responder. It is especially important to plan in the tax area because of the many types of taxes you have.

TYPES OF TAXES

It has been rightly said that you are taxed when you earn, you are taxed when you spend, you are taxed when you give, you are taxed when your investments do well, and you are taxed when you die. As a matter of fact, you are taxed almost any time there is a money transaction.

Some of the many kinds of taxes that you pay are:

- *Income taxes*—Federal, state, city, and county taxes on income earned.
- *Sales taxes*—Taxes imposed by state and local communities on sales of all types of goods and services.
- *Intangible taxes*—Taxes on various intangible properties owned, usually including stocks, bonds, and other investments. This tax is generally imposed by state governments.
- *Use taxes*—Taxes for the use of goods and services provided by taxing authorities, such as gasoline taxes for the use of roads and airport taxes for the use of airports.
- *Estate taxes*—Taxes imposed by the federal government on the accumulation of material wealth when a person dies.
- *Inheritance taxes*—Taxes imposed by state and local governments, again, on estates accumulated.
- *Gift taxes*—Taxes imposed on the transfer of various kinds of property to another person. Gift taxes and estate taxes are typi-

cally referred to as transfer taxes. In other words, the transferring of property from one person to another results in a tax.

* *Property taxes*—Taxes imposed by local authorities on property owned.
* *Social Security taxes*—Taxes imposed by the federal government on wages, earnings, and self-employment income to pay for social security benefits.

This list is not meant to be all-inclusive, but merely to illustrate that you do pay taxes at almost every turn of your financial life. In this chapter I will discuss tax planning in the area of income taxes at the state and federal levels only. In Chapter 14, I will deal with transfer taxes. None of the other taxes will be covered in this book, because they are basically non-controllable, except as they relate to other spending decisions.

INCOME TAX RATES

Two terms must be understood before we discuss tax planning: marginal tax rates and effective tax rates or, stated another way, marginal tax brackets and effective tax brackets. When people say they are in a 15% tax bracket, they mean that their next dollar of income is taxed at the 15% level or, conversely, that their next dollar of tax deduction reduces taxes by fifteen cents.

The graduated income tax system in the United States means that various levels of income are taxed at different rates. As the income reaches a higher level, the rate goes up, but, and this is important to remember, *the rate does not go up on all of the previously earned and taxed income*—it only applies to that level. For illustrative purposes I have constructed a hypothetical tax table as follows:

Chart 12–A

(1) If Taxable Income is	(2) Tax on Column 1	(3) Tax on Excess
$10,000	$ 1,000	12%
20,000	2,200	15%
30,000	3,700	20%
40,000	5,700	30%

The illustration is clearer when we define some terms.

Taxable Income. Taxable income is the portion of your earned income that is ultimately taxed after taking into account all deductions, exemptions, and other reductions due to investments, IRA's, and the like.

Column 3 gives the tax bracket, and it is the percentage applied to the *last* dollar of taxable income. In other words, if the taxable income in this illustration is any place between $10,001 and $20,000, the tax bracket is 12%, the percent paid on the last dollar of income.

Marginal Rate. This determines the amount that will be paid on the *next* dollar of income that cannot be offset with a deduction. If a person currently has taxable income of $30,000 and he earns one more dollar of income, that dollar of income is taxed at 20%. Therefore, his marginal rate is 20%, and that stays 20% until his taxable income reaches $40,001, at which time the marginal rate to be paid goes to 30%. The marginal rate and the tax bracket could be the same, but won't always be. The tax bracket is determined by the *last dollar* of the taxable income, and the marginal rate is determined by the *next dollar* of taxable income.

Effective Rate. This is the total amount paid in taxes divided by the total income earned. In the case of Bob and Laura, they earned $34,600 last year. However, they were allowed exemptions for themselves and their children, as well as itemized deductions for medical expenses, property taxes, state income taxes, charitable contributions, and so on. All of these deductions and exemptions reduce the total income down to the taxable income. The income taxes are then computed on taxable income.

If we assume that their taxable income was $20,000, then the taxes that they would pay on the $20,000 is $2,200, which represents 6.36% of the total income of $34,600. Therefore, we can say that even though they are in the 12% tax bracket and will marginally pay 15%, they are effectively paying only 6.36% of their income in taxes. *The effective rate is the key number.* It is much more important than the tax bracket or marginal rate.

> *The simple objective in tax planning is to reduce the effective tax rate in order to generate after-tax dollars for any goals that you have.*

Living expenses, debt retirement, and investments are three categories of cash flow requirements that are paid with after-tax dollars in
almost every case. Therefore, if the objective is to pay zero taxes, all
living expenses, debt retirement, and many investments must be paid
with either borrowed funds or not paid at all.

For example, if Bob and Laura decide to pay off their home mortgage
of $40,000, that means over time they must generate, after taxes,
$40,000 with which to pay that debt. There is no way they can pay the
debt with pretax dollars. By the same token, if their objective is to have
$20,000 of living expenses this year, then they must generate, after
taxes, after giving, and after debt repayment, $20,000. The lower the
effective tax rate, the more easily this is accomplished. However, that
rate can never go to zero, as I previously explained. The question is,
How can you reduce your effective tax rate? Remember, the effective
rate is far more important than the tax bracket or marginal rate.

TAX PLANNING STRATEGIES

The most popular time for tax planning by taxpayers is December,
with the second most popular month being April. However, both
months are too late to do any serious tax planning. Once December 31st
has passed, nothing can be done, other than an IRA or pension plan
investment, to reduce taxes for the previous year. Most people know this
and become rather panicky in the month of December, wondering how
they are going to reduce their taxes. My general rule for tax planning is:

> *The shorter the perspective on tax planning, the higher
> the risk that must be taken and/or the fewer the options
> that are available.*

I believe that most income tax planning should be done at least one
year in advance with monitoring and the necessary adjustments made
in the plan at least quarterly during the year. This means that the tax
planning you do on December 31st would *not* be for the current year,
but for the next year, so that you are always one year ahead. Tax planning is much like a funnel—at the beginning of the year, the options are
many, but as you go through the year, the funnel narrows and the op-

tions become fewer. As a stream of liquid passing through the funnel rushes more rapidly near the nozzle, so the emotional intensity increases as the year goes by. The end of the year, with so few options available and so much emotion being generated, is the time when many poor tax planning decisions are made.

All tax planning falls into four general tax planning strategies: timing, shifting, investing, and use of the tax law. You don't need to be an expert to understand these four general strategies, but you need merely to ask yourself four questions:

1. *Timing.* Can I reduce my taxes by changing the year I am to receive income or to pay deductible expenses in?
2. *Shifting.* Can I reduce my taxes by shifting my income to someone in my family who is in a lower tax bracket?
3. *Investing.* Can I reduce my taxes through the use of investments?
4. *Use of Tax Law.* Can I reduce my taxes through the wise use of any additional tax law provisions that I am not now using?

1. TIMING STRATEGIES

Timing strategies involve the timing of the recognition of income and the deduction of expenses. The general rule is that you should always push income into a future year and pull expenses into the current year. Why? Because, even if it does not change the tax bracket one way or the other, the utilization of a timing strategy does delay the payment of taxes. For example, if a taxpayer is in the 15% tax bracket and has the opportunity to delay $1,000 of income, it will reduce the current taxes by $150; but because that income went into the next year, it increases the taxes paid next year by $150. That may not seem to make any difference; however, the taxpayer, not the government, has had the use of $150 for one year and the time to earn interest on that $150. Previously, we saw how a little bit over a long time period can add up to a great deal through the magic of compounding.

Pulling deductions into the current year has the same effect. For example, if a taxpayer is in the 15% tax bracket and pulls $1,000 of deductions from next year into this year, the tax liability goes down $150 for the current year and up $150 for the next year. As above, this strategy enables the taxpayer to control the $150 for a longer time.

In considering this strategy, the doctrine in tax law called the doctrine of "Constructive Receipt" must be understood. The doctrine of Constructive Receipt simply says that if you earn the income and have a right to receive it, you cannot postpone the taxes incurred on that amount by merely choosing not to receive it.

For example, a person offering professional services receives checks near the end of the year, but in an effort to avoid taxable income, he merely sticks them in a bottom drawer and does not deposit them until after December 31st. This violates the doctrine of Constructive Receipt. He is attempting to use a timing strategy in reducing his income, but as a matter of fact, it is tax evasion, not tax avoidance.

There are many legal ways to defer income, such as postponing the work that would generate the income so that the payment received for it is not due until the following year. Also, money invested in a savings type of account, such as a money market fund, is taxed, as the interest is earned on a daily basis. Instead of leaving the money in such an account, invest it in a Treasury Bill that has a maturity date beyond the end of the year. Then the income generated by that investment is taxed in the subsequent year rather than the current year.

A self-employed person can choose to pay bonuses after the end of the calendar year, thereby postponing the tax on that income until the next year. There are other ways to defer income, but my objective here is to challenge your thinking and your own creativity rather than to provide a tax manual.

Some of the obvious ways to pull deductions into the current year are to pay for all expenses incurred, but not yet paid, prior to the end of the year—for example, interest on debt that has been incurred, medical expenses that have been incurred but not yet paid, legal fees, state income taxes, and so on. You cannot, according to the law, prepay interest and medical expenses, but you can bring the payments up to date, thereby deducting them in the current year as opposed to the subequent year. You will need to be alert for these deductions as delayed billing in December is increasingly common by professionals.

My recommendation is that you review last year's tax return and ask yourself the question for each item of income, Could it have been deferred into the subsequent year? And for each deduction you took, ask yourself the question, Could I have pulled more deductions in this area from the subsequent year? Because of their nature, timing strategies are about the only strategies that work near the end of the year. Almost all of the other strategies must be implemented earlier in the year.

2. SHIFTING STRATEGIES

Understanding tax brackets is essential for understanding shifting strategies. The shifting strategies ask the question, Can I shift what would be taxable income to me to a taxpaying entity in a lower tax bracket? For example, can I shift income from my wife and me, who are in a high tax bracket, to our children, who are in a very low tax bracket, and perhaps pay no taxes at all. The assumption in using this type of strategy is that I can shift the income and either still retain control of that income or use it for an item that I would have paid for anyway.

Probably the classic example of shifting income is in the area of providing for the college education of children. Many times parents will have the opportunity to give their children income-producing assets so that the child can pay the income taxes earned on that income rather than the parent and use the income left over, after paying taxes, to pay for a college education.

For example, if the college education costs are $5,000 per year and the parents are paying that cost, they must earn the $5,000 plus the taxes on that $5,000 in order to have $5,000 left over to pay for the college education. If their tax bracket is 27%, then they must earn approximately $6,849 to have $5,000 left over with which to pay education costs. If, on the other hand, the child is in the 15% tax bracket, he or she can earn $5,882, pay the taxes, and still have $5,000 left over. The parents, then, have paid for the college education for that year with substantially fewer dollars than had they paid the taxes on their earnings and then funded the college education with after-tax earnings.

The shifting strategy typically works best within a family. The reason this strategy works best within families is that the ultimate objective is not to give away money, but to reduce taxes on income that is earned. You could, for example, give me $10,000 of income-producing assets (which, incidentally, I would gladly accept). However, you are out-of-pocket for the total gift, and even though your income taxes went down, this did not make good economic sense.

Gifting

There are three primary ways that the shifting strategy works. First of all, income may be shifted by *gifting* to another family member income-producing assets, such as real estate, stocks, bonds, closely held stock and notes, or mortgages receivable. The only problem is that a gift literally must be made and the property legally transferred to the other person. It cannot be loaned to them, nor transferred under any type of facade. A gift must actually be made, and if the gift is large enough, a gift tax may have to be paid. For this reason, a second method of shifting income is used by many.

Trusts

Various trusts can be established that can shift income to another, but the ultimate control or ownership of the property transferred is retained. The most common trust used to accomplish this technique is what is called the Clifford Trust or the Ten-year Trust. Simply speaking, property can be transferred into a Clifford Trust set up by the taxpayer whereby the income earned by the trust is taxed either to the trust at a lower rate, or to the beneficiaries of the trust, most typically a child, at a lower rate. At the end of ten years, the property that was originally transferred into the trust reverts to the original owner. However, the property cannot be taken out of the trust during that ten-year time period, and during that ten-year time period, the income does go to the trust beneficiaries. This type of trust does not work nearly as well under the new tax reform act. However, it is still an alternative to be considered.

In some cases, property can be transferred to what is known as a Charitable Lead Trust whereby the income from that property goes to a charity, and the property, at the end of the term of the trust, either reverts to the original owner or to someone of their designation. This is a very complex trust with many tax and personal ramifications, and a legal expert needs to be consulted before entering into this type of situation. Many Christian organizations have experts in the area of estates and trusts who can help you accomplish the objective of reducing your taxes by shifting your income but still retaining ultimate control over the property.

Each of the techniques described—gifting and the use of trusts—requires substantial legal and other expenses. Additionally, there is always a loss of control of the dollars involved, and as a consequence, it is vitally important to consult a professional before considering any of these techniques. My objective here has simply been to get you to consider these techniques—not necessarily to give you the counsel that would enable you to use them wisely.

3. INVESTMENTS

The basis of every investment you make is to produce more value or more income over time. Income from investments is taxed in various ways and can, therefore, have a great impact on total taxes paid. Income investments are taxed in four ways.

Tax-exempt

The income from some investments, such as municipal bonds, is tax exempt by law, and as a result, this income is substantially lower than the fully taxable income earned on similar types of investments.

Tax-deferred

Some investments require that no tax be paid on the income earned until some time in the future. Almost all pension plans fall into this category, whether it is an employer-only contribution or one of your own pension plans such as an IRA, a Keogh plan, or a qualified retirement plan. In addition, tax deferred annuities sold by brokerage houses and insurance companies allow you to accumulate on a tax-deferred basis.

The value of a tax deferred investment is that compounding works for you not only on your portion of the income earned on the investment but also on the portion that would have gone to pay taxes, had they not been deferred. Additionally, when it is time to pay taxes on the investment income that has been generated, presumably the investor is retired and in a lower tax bracket and, therefore, in real dollar terms, pays less in income taxes.

Tax-favored

Tax-favored investments are investments having special income tax allowances and provisions, again merely as a matter of law and not because of the nature of the investment. For example, most oil and gas tax investments enjoy a favored status due to the depletion allowance.

Fully Taxable

The fourth type of investment is one that is fully taxable and includes almost all interest-bearing types of investments other than those described above.

The principle still needs to be remembered that anytime there is a favorable tax consequence to an investment, there is a corresponding cost somewhere. For example, in the tax-exempt investments, the cost is that the yield is not as high as in fully taxable investments. In the case of tax-deferred investments, the cost is the nonliquidity of the investment owing to the penalties associated with withdrawing the monies. In the area of tax-favored investments, the cost is typically in the higher risk associated with those investments.

To give you an idea of the consequences of the taxability of income and what that means in terms of your ability to accumulate, the following chart assumes a $1,000 investment per year. The tax-free investment return is 5%; the tax-deferred investment return is 8%; the fully taxable return, also at 8%, is assumed at a 25% marginal tax rate.

In reviewing the chart, it is easy to see that the tax bracket you are in has a major bearing on the relative attractiveness of the investment. At

Chart 12–B

	5% Tax-free	8% Yield Tax-deferred	8% Yield 25% Tax Bracket
Year 1	$ 1,050	$ 1,080	$ 1,060
Year 5	5,525	5,867	5,637
Year 10	12,578	14,487	13,181
Year 15	21,579	27,152	23,276
Year 20	33,067	45,762	36,786
Year 25	47,727	73,106	54,864
Year 30	66,439	113,283	79,058
Year 35	90,320	172,317	111,435
Year 40	127,800	295,056	154,762
Years the fund will last if it continues to earn interest but a withdrawal of $29,500 per year is made	5.0	22.0	6.5

the end of 40 years in the tax deferred investment, you could begin drawing an amount at 10% per year and would have both a return of principal and income in terms of the taxable consequence of that withdrawal. If we assume the withdrawal is 10% per year and that all of the withdrawal is interest and fully taxable and the remaining fund continues to earn 8%, the tax-deferred fund is still not depleted until *22 years* in the future. Compare this to withdrawing the same $29,500 from the other funds, which results in total depletion of the tax-free fund after five years, of the fully taxable fund at the 25% tax rate in 6.5 years.

As you anticipate the end of your accumulation, the tax-free nature of certain income may appear desirable. However, the illustration shows the value of compounding on a tax-deferred basis as compared to any other alternative. Tax-free investments do not yield enough to offset the compounding impact on a tax-deferred basis, nor do they offset the compounding associated with fully taxable amounts for the taxpayer in the 25% bracket in this illustration.

The primary point is that there are different types of tax-favored investments. When making an investment decision, the decision, first of all, is an investment decision and, second, a tax decision. However, the taxes can make one more favorable than another.

4. USE OF TAX LAW PROVISIONS

The last strategy to use in tax planning is to review all the tax law provisions that allow for deductions, deferrals, credits, and the like to make sure you are using all that are applicable to your situation. These provisions are somewhat technical and fill pages of the Internal Revenue Code, so I will explain only the major categories, and then in each category, list some of the tax law provisions that might be applicable. Review these and seek advice from a professional if you think they are applicable.

Adjustments to Income

Adjustments to income are just exactly that—certain expenditures that adjust the income reported on the tax form in order to compute what is called "adjusted gross income." Adjusted gross income is an important number because some deductions on the tax return relate to that number. The most common adjustments allowable to income are moving expenses, employee business expenses, IRA payments, and Keogh payments.

Itemized Deductions

Some itemized deductions that are allowable are medical and dental expenses; state and local taxes, including property taxes, income taxes, and all personal property taxes; certain interest paid; charitable contributions of either cash or property.

I am often asked whether contributions of time are deductible, and the answer is no. If you do not receive income for the time spent, you already have received, in effect, a deduction by not having the income to report as taxable income.

The most commonly overlooked itemized deductions are:

- Expenses paid as a volunteer for charitable organizations
- Points paid on a purchase of a personal residence
- Personal property taxes

Tax Credits

In addition to deductions and adjustments to income, tax law provides for tax credits that reduce taxes dollar-for-dollar, whereas adjustments and deductions do not.

Tax credits include the foreign tax credits, if you pay taxes in a foreign country, child and dependent care credit for expenses paid by a working couple, and certain limited investment tax credits for energy, property, and rehabilitation expenditures.

Special Provisions

In addition, the IRS has special provisions for certain situations such as the deferral of the tax on the gain from the sale of a principal residence, exemptions for each dependent, and for many, many other situations and items.

Using the tax law provisions typically requires expert counsel, but you should review the tax return package sent to you by the government very thoroughly. The preparation of the tax return is distasteful for most of us, and therefore we fail to pay close enough attention to all of the provisions that will help us reduce our taxes.

Special Opportunity

Ours is the only country in the world that allows charitable deductions for income tax purposes. One of the principal advantages that our government allows in this area is the deduction of the full fair market value of a gift of property. For example, if you had purchased a stock for $10,000 and it had appreciated in value to $20,000, and if you sold that stock and paid the tax on it of, say, $2,700, you would have $17,300 left to give to a charitable organization. The $17,300 contribution would further reduce your taxes by (for illustration purposes) 27% or $4,671, so that the net cost to making the charitable contribution would be the $20,000 property less the $4,671 tax savings or $15,329.

If, on the other hand, the stock had been contributed directly to the charitable organization, there would have been a $20,000 contribution allowed, with a tax savings of $5,400, for a net cost of $14,600. The charity, in turn, could sell the property for $20,000 and have $20,000 rather than $17,300, and it would have cost the taxpayer $729 less $5,400–$4,671 to give a charity $2,700 more ($20,000–$17,300). Obviously, this is a "win-win" situation. The following chart illustrates this opportunity for taxpayers in various tax brackets:

Chart 12–C

GIVE CASH

	15% Tax Bracket	35% Tax Bracket	27% Tax Bracket
Sales Price	$20,000	$20,000	$20,000
Tax or Gain	(1,500)	(3,900)	(2,700)
Given to Charities	18,500	16,500	17,300
Tax Savings	$ 2,775	$ 5,775	$ 4,671
Cost to Giver:			
Stock Value	$20,000	$20,000	$20,000
Less Tax Savings	(2,775)	(5,775)	(4,671)
Actual Cost	$17,225	$14,225	$15,329

GIVE PROPERTY

Given to Charity	$20,000	$20,000	$20,000
Tax Savings	(3,000)	(7,500)	(5,400)
Actual Cost	$17,000	$12,500	$14,600
Difference	$ 225	$ 1,725	$ 729

ACTION TO BE TAKEN

As a taxpayer you need to take three steps. First, determine the projected tax liability for the following year as early in the year as possible; second, plan to reduce that liability through the many items discussed here; and third, set the withholding amount and tax estimate amount at the projected liability amount.

No taxpayer has to pay more than his last year's liability or his current year's liability, whichever one is less. Again, as I said earlier, to receive a tax refund is a sign of poor planning. I recommend that you determine your projected tax liability simply by taking last year's tax return and projecting to the best of your knowledge what the numbers will be this year. Use the chart on page 174.

After doing this, determine the withholding amounts paid to date, for the year, compared to what will be paid in if the withholdings stay at the same level. If needed, you can adjust the withholding to the newly determined amount. Last year over 72 million people got an average refund of $850. In effect, what they had done was make an interest-free loan to the government for $850 for one year.

In Bob and Laura's case, they determined that by changing their W–4 to reduce withholdings to the rate that coincides with what they would actually receive, they could generate an additional $2,500 of cash flow this year. Additionally, they need to make a decision about whether or not to do an IRA for both of them. Laura has $2,000 of self-employment income, which could be used to fund an IRA, and of course Bob could, also. Because they do not have the excess cash flow to do so, they would have to decide whether that money should come out of their savings account. The chances are that they should, but we will discuss that option for them in the next chapter.

Chart 12–D

INCOME TAX ANALYSIS

	Last Year	Estimated This Year
INCOME:		
Salary	————	————
Interest & Dividends	————	————
Business Income (Schedule C)	————	————
State Tax Refund	————	————
Schedule D Income	————	————
Schedule E Income	————	————
Other	————	————
GROSS INCOME	————	————
LESS ADJUSTMENTS TO INCOME:		
IRA/Keogh	————	————
Business Expenses	————	————
Married Couple Deduction	————	————
Other	————	————
Adjusted Gross Income	═══	═══
LESS ITEMIZED DEDUCTIONS:		
Medical Expenses	————	————
Taxes	————	————
Interest	————	————
Contributions	————	————
Miscellaneous	————	————
Less Zero Bracket	(————)	(————)
Total Deductions	═══	═══
LESS EXEMPTIONS	————	————
TAXABLE INCOME	═══	═══
FEDERAL INCOME TAX	————	————
PLUS OTHER TAXES:		
Self-employment Tax	————	————
Other	————	————
LESS CREDITS	(————)	(————)
TOTAL FEDERAL TAX	————	————
TOTAL STATE TAX	————	————
TOTAL TAX	═══	═══
MARGINAL TAX RATE	═══	═══
EFFECTIVE TAX RATE	═══	═══

CONCLUSION

Tax planning must be integrated with all other types of planning. However, tax planning should not be the "tail that wags the dog"; it should rather remain the tail. Investment planning requires, first of all, that you make a good investment and then consider the tax consequences, rather than make the investment for tax consequences. That goes for charitable contributions, estate planning, and any other type of financial decision.

Tax planning is very important, but it is not a panacea for cash flow problems. Every decision that causes a reduction in taxes, has a corresponding cost associated with it. Therefore, reducing taxes may increase cash flow in the short term, but there is a cost associated with it, and that must be considered. Just remember, there is no "free lunch," especially in the cafeteria of tax reductions.

13

Investment Planning

PEOPLE TEND TO think that since I am a Christian financial planner I am against acquiring material possessions or accumulations. Once when Judy and I were with a couple, the woman showed us a very large diamond she was wearing, and then quickly explained that the diamond was an "investment." I smiled and wondered to myself how high the price of diamonds would have to go before that diamond would be sold. My opinion is that the diamond would not be taken off the woman's finger at any price.

An investment is something that is purchased with the intent to resell at a higher price. Therefore, diamonds, expensive cars, vacation homes, antiques, and the like, never qualify as investments. They are purchases that may go up in value and consequently prove to be a wise purchase, but they are not investments. Many people delude themselves into calling a purchase an investment in order to justify its purchase, but it is never an investment unless it was purchased with one objective in mind: to preserve or increase its value and, ultimately, to resell it at a higher price than what was paid for it.

It is *critical* that you understand the difference between an investment and a purchase because different criteria are used to evaluate each one. In this chapter, we will only be dealing with investments—things purchased solely either to generate a yield to the investor or to grow in value, or to do both. If they are not accomplishing the intended objective, then they should be sold immediately.

MOST COMMON INVESTMENT MISTAKES

I am in the enviable position of representing clients who, for the most part, have fairly significant sums of discretionary dollars each year to invest. As such, they are approached regularly with "good deals," and our firm is constantly barraged with good deals to present to our clients.

Obviously, not all of these deals are good deals. But on the front end, they always seem to be. Good deals only become bad deals over time, and I have learned something: *There will be as good a deal tomorrow as there is today*. Therefore, I never have to respond to the "good deal" that is presented to me today regardless of how good it is, because my experience has shown that I will have another one tomorrow and another one the next day, and another one the next day, and another one the next day.

I call this dilemma the "binary trap." The binary trap centers on the question, Should I do this or not? It only gives me two alternatives—yes or no—and if the deal is a good deal I most certainly should say yes to it. However, the binary trap begs the real question, What is the best use of these discretionary funds? When I ask the question that way, I immediately open up many more alternatives to investing than just the one presented.

Unless there is a long-term investment strategy in place, you will always be subject to falling into the binary trap. The best investment for any investor depends upon one's personal long-term goals and the strategy to accomplish those goals. Then any investment that comes along is selected as a means to meet the goals in light of the strategy, as opposed to assuming that every good investment is something that everyone should participate in.

Rather than looking at specific investments (a major topic that needs to be covered in a separate book), I feel it is more important for you to develop and to understand your strategy. Then individual investments, as they come along, can be evaluated in light of your strategy rather than the reverse—setting your strategy on the basis of the investments you have made.

From an investment standpoint, we have basically two time periods of life. The time period when we are accumulating to meet long-term goals I simply call *the accumulation phase*. In this phase of life we are accumulating not only material possessions but also investments for the purpose of accomplishing our long-term goals of financial independence, starting our own business, and the like.

Once the long-term goals have been met, and we have accumulated enough by that definition, we enter the second phase of investing—*the preservation phase*. In the preservation phase we want to preserve the assets we have accumulated in light of the various risks that we face, such as inflation, deflation, monetary collapse, interest rates going up and down, and the like.

Figure 13.1 illustrates these two time periods of an investor's life. Basically, from age 20 to approximately age 40, we are accumulating material possessions, paying off debt, and raising our families. The major accumulation begins to take place between the ages of 40 and 50, and at some point during this time period we cross the line of having accumulated enough to meet our long-term goals. However, almost no one stops accumulating at this point for one very good reason—the uncertainty of our economic environment. Some time around the age of 60, we shift to a preservation mode where we are attempting to preserve our assets in light of the risks.

Then at some point between 60 and 80, we enter the distribution phase. The distribution phase of investment planning can be either immediate, in the event of death, or planned to take place over a long term. We will discuss the distribution phase of life in Chapter 14 on estate planning.

Obviously, the graph will be different for different people. Some of us achieve our long-term goals very early; others of us never achieve our long-term goals. The point is to understand where you are and what that

Figure 13.1

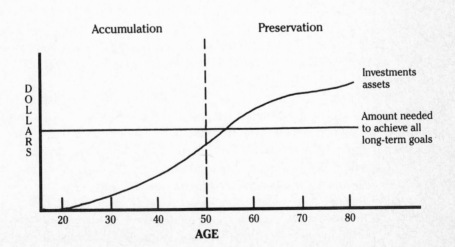

means for your investment strategy. You need to know if you are in an accumulation strategy or a preservation strategy because the investment techniques and the type of investment to be considered are different for each of the strategies.

It is also important to know what level of accumulation (represented by the line on the graph) is needed to meet the long-term goals. That number and that line define how much is enough. When you go beyond that line, you have to answer the question, Why am I continuing to accumulate?

The two key questions to ask yourself when considering investing and an investment strategy are: (1) Why am I investing? (What long-term goal will this investment help to meet?) and (2) What is my strategy—accumulation or preservation?

ACCUMULATION STRATEGY

The basic philosophy that I have been attempting to communicate throughout this book is that a little bit over a long time period will allow you to accomplish your long-term goals. The alternative is to get rich quick and live with the high risk of losing it all. Most persons invest by responding rather than planning. I hope by this point you are convinced that planning your investments, rather than responding to the alternatives presented to you, is a far more secure path to achieving your long-term financial goals.

First of all, the accumulation strategy revolves around having a cash flow margin and then making a decision regarding the use of this margin. You say, "The best use of this margin is _____."
The "best" will depend on four things—your personal goals, the commitments you already have, your personal priorities, and all the other alternatives for spending this margin.

I have a recommendation for the sequential use of your cash flow margin, and I call it the Sequential Accumulation Strategy. With this investment strategy, you use the first dollar of cash flow margin to accomplish Step 1, and all additional dollars of margin to accomplish each step in sequence. The strategy is as follows:

Step 1: Eliminate all credit card and consumer debt. This, as explained earlier, provides an immediate "investment return" of 12% to 21%. Not having to pay that interest cost each year is, in effect, the same as achieving the same rate of return on any monies invested by you.

Therefore, it is the surest and highest form of investment return you can make.

Step 2: Set aside one month's living expenses in the checking account. This is in addition to the current month's living expenses that are in the checking account, so at the beginning of any one month there would be two month's living expenses already deposited in the checking account. This "investment" is for flexibility.

Step 3: Invest between two and six months' living expenses in an interest-bearing money market fund account. This becomes the emergency fund and, in effect, your own bank. As you need money to make a major purchase or have an unexpected major expense or see an opportunity to save through purchasing now instead of later, you can borrow from yourself out of this account rather than from a lending institution. Once the money has been borrowed, it should, of course, be replaced. Steps 2 and 3 provide you with flexibility so that you will be guarded against emergencies that come up that might totally drain your resources.

Step 4: Save in an interest-bearing account for major purchases. This is the planned purchase of major items such as automobiles, furniture, and even the downpayment on a home.

Steps 1 through 4 should be done in sequence rather than all at once. In other words, you do not go to Step 3 until you have accomplished Step 2. By doing so, you eliminate the need to make a decision whenever an investment alternative comes to you. If you have not already accomplished Steps 1 through 4, you let the option go by.

Step 5: Accumulate to meet long-term goals. The long-term goals of financial independence, college education, giving, owning your own business, paying off debt, and major lifestyle changes, as depicted in your financial planning diagram, are now funded through various investment alternatives. These investment alternatives, however, will have one characteristic—they will be almost risk-free because you are still accumulating to meet your long-term goals and therefore have no dollars left with which to speculate.

Step 6: Use investment dollars to speculate in higher risk investments. At this point, by definition, every short-term and long-term goal has already been met. I have seen very few people ever reach this step of investing, and coincidentally, those who have, don't like to speculate because they don't want to risk the loss. They prefer to adopt what I have called the "preservation investment strategy."

Figure 13.2

SEQUENTIAL INVESTMENT STRATEGY

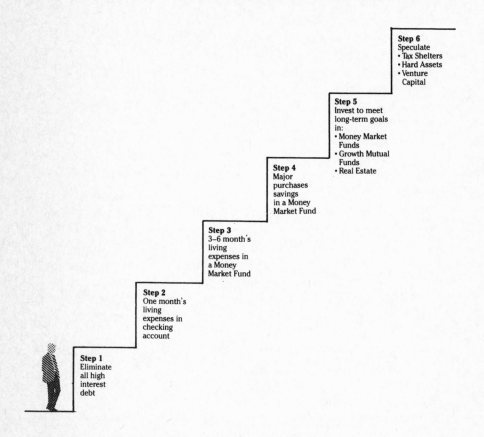

Let me repeat that the sequential investment strategy is totally dependent upon having a positive cash flow margin. As you have a positive cash flow, the first priority use of that cash is Step 1, and so forth in sequence. This sequence obviously represents my opinion about what the priorities should be; your priorities may be different. For example, Step 4 may be a higher priority for you than my Step 3, and that is perfectly acceptable. The important point is to prayerfully set your priorities and to have a strategy for meeting them.

You may even decide to do your investing concurrently rather than sequentially. I believe Steps 1 and 2 must be met first, but then Steps 3, 4, and 5 could be met concurrently with the cash flow margin for the year allocated in the following way:

To Step 3—	40%	30%		?%
To Step 4—	40%	or 60%	or	?%
To Step 5—	20%	10%		?%
Total	100%	100%		100%

Do not forget your strategy and become involved in premature investing and speculation.

TOOLS AND TECHNIQUES

In addition to understanding specific investment products, such as stocks, bonds, T-Bills, gold, silver, land, mutual funds, apartments, and the like, you need to know the tools and techniques for investing these specific products. For example, an IRA is a *tool* allowed by the government and basically the same type of tool as any pension plan. Dollar cost averaging, which is a strategy of committing a fixed amount of money per month to a particular investment resulting in a low per unit cost, is a *technique* of investing. Market timing is a *technique* of buying and selling stocks or mutual funds according to a mathematical formula resulting one hopes, over time, in selling near the top of the market and buying near the bottom of the market.

Each of these tools and/or techniques uses one of the specific investment products to accomplish its objective. The techniques require a great deal of experience and expertise to be effective and should be utilized by the investor only with assistance by an expert. The tools, such as an IRA, require merely that the investor know whether the tool fits his or her situation and then how to implement the tool through the use of one of the products.

The tools and techniques can be used either during the accumulation or the preservation phase of investing.

SPECIFIC INVESTMENTS

For those who are still accumulating, I recommend three primary types of investments:

1. Money Market Instruments

These investment products are liquid and yielding with very little risk of loss of principal except in an inflationary time. Specifically, these investments would include certificates of deposit, Treasury Bills, savings accounts, and money market funds. Money market funds or mutual funds with a brokerage house are typically better than money market accounts in a bank because they have fewer restrictions.

The advantage of a money market fund type of investment or any other short-term, interest-bearing investment is that you have professional money managers managing your investment in order to achieve the highest return at the lowest risk while maintaining total liquidity of the investment. Therefore, you don't have to guess about whether interest rates are going up or down, and you always have the opportunity to move the money out of the money market fund if a better alternative investment comes along.

2. Mutual Funds

A mutual fund is, in effect, a pooled fund of money from many investors that is entrusted to a professional money manager. There are almost as many types of mutual funds as there are investment objectives. The three main types are: long-term growth funds that invest primarily in the stock market, income funds that invest basically in high yielding types of investments, and a combination of income and growth funds that attempt to achieve both objectives.

The advantage of using mutual funds for accumulation is that you achieve professional management, diversification in your investments, total liquidity of the funds, and you can choose a fund that fits your specific goals, such as growth or income.

Various mutual funds are evaluated in many periodicals. As you gain information and expertise, you can make mutual fund switches since they are very easy to get into and out of. There are even families of funds that allow you to switch your objectives within the same mutual fund. It is fairly easy to determine, given the objectives that you have, which mutual funds meet those objectives.

3. Real Estate Investments

This type of accumulation investment is comprised of either personally owned rental type real estate or public real estate partnerships. Personally owned real estate can typically take a great deal of experience and time with a fairly high risk, especially for the novice. On the other hand, you can invest in public real estate partnerships for as little as $1,000 to $5,000 and still accomplish the goals of growth through real estate without having a substantial sum of money or expertise. Once investors move into private placement real estate investments and other investments such as oil and gas, tax shelters, gold and silver, first and second mortgages, my recommendation is that they always use an expert counselor to choose the specific investment.

PRESERVATION INVESTMENT STRATEGY

The perfect investment is one that is totally liquid, with no risk, yielding a high percentage of return, and growing at a rate greater than the inflation rate. I have yet to see the perfect investment because there are always trade-offs. An investment that is liquid typically does not grow in value—for example, a savings account. On the other hand, one that is growing in value, such as real estate, probably bears some risk, may not have a yield associated with it, and certainly is not liquid.

A good investment strategy for *the entire investment portfolio* accomplishes four specifically quantified universal investment objectives: (1) maximize liquidity, (2) maximize growth, (3) maximize yield, and (4) minimize risk. Of these four objectives, investors will have different priorities that are dependent upon a variety of things.

Age. A younger person needs less liquidity, takes more risk, needs more growth, and can accept less yield.

Temperament. Some people can stand no risk and want all of their money invested in certificates of deposit. Others have the philosophy, "Let's roll the dice."

Tax situation. Those in the higher tax brackets are more typically concerned with growth than they are yield because the tax on the growth is deferred, whereas yield is typically taxed in the current higher income tax brackets.

Other financial commitments. A debt may need to be repaid in the near future or lifestyle commitments for the near future may require more liquidity than at other times.

Certainty of future cash flow. Some people have a certainty of future cash flow through pension plans, other retirement plans, Social Security, and the like, and the yield factor is less important for them than the growth factor. Others may have no retirement income, and therefore the yield factor is far more important to them.

The point is that each of these four universal investment objectives can be quantified, dependent upon your age, temperament, tax situation, personal philosophy, perception, and goals. Then an investment portfolio can be designed that is measurable in terms of its ability to accomplish the objectives that have been set.

Types of Risk

Once the investment portfolio has been designed and its ability to meet the universal investment objectives measured, an evaluation of the "risk" in the portfolio needs to be done. It used to be simple to define risk as merely the loss of principal. Money stored or hidden stood the risk of thieves and erosion, whereas money invested in a bank stood the risk of bank failures. However, for the most part, the risk was well-known and could be planned for. Once an investment portfolio becomes sizeable and once we introduce a worldwide and a very uncertain economic situation, the risks become far more complex and more difficult to plan for. For example:

1. *A business risk.* Some investments such as a real estate project or a specific stock are dependent upon the successful running of a business in order for the principal to remain intact.

2. *A financial risk.* Some investments will retain their relative value in times of monetary collapse or total economic or political upheaval whereas others won't. For example, during a monetary collapse, real estate and gold may retain their relative value whereas cash probably will not. Many investments, therefore, bear some financial risk.

3. *Market risks.* No one has total control of the market; rather we are subject to whatever market we happen to be investing in, whether it is the real estate market or the stock market or the bond market. Any investment that is a part of a larger market bears a risk that is basically uncontrollable by any one individual.

4. *Interest rate risk.* Many investments will provide a current interest rate, but if that interest rate is fixed and interest rates for similar types of investments go up, you have borne an interest rate risk. As an investment strategy, it used to be safe to invest in long-term, nontaxable municipal bonds yielding 3%, 4%, 5%, or 6%. The interest rate was known, and if you then locked that interest rate in for a long time period, you were relatively safe.

Obviously, the seventies have shown us that the interest rate risk can be substantial. We saw many investment yields go to 18%, 19%, and 20%, and those who had locked up their investments for long time periods at much lower rates lost the opportunity to earn the higher interest rates.

5. *Purchasing power risk.* Investments in cash type investments, such as certificates of deposit, money market funds, savings accounts, Treasury Bills, among other instruments, experience a loss in purchasing power during times of inflation, whereas in times of deflation, they experience an increase in purchasing power.

6. *Tax risk.* Many investments, such as tax shelters, have a risk of future assessments associated with them because the IRS may change the law or their interpretation of the law. An investment in cash probably bears no tax risk, whereas an investment in an opal mine in Brazil, yielding a five to one tax write-off, might bear a substantial tax risk.

7. *Legal risks.* Certain investments may have a risk of lawsuits associated with them. For example, if you are investing in rental real estate, you certainly bear the risk of a lawsuit if someone is injured on your property.

There are three ways to reduce the risk taken in any one investment or on the whole investment portfolio. First of all, become personally knowledgeable about investments and the risk you are taking before entering into an investment. Second, use experts since no one can be an expert in everything. However, the burden of taking the risk is always on the investor rather than on the advisor.

Third, do not attempt to guess the future, but rather diversify your investments so that some will be worth more over time while others will be worth less over time, depending on changing economic situations. If all investments have been properly diversified, the overall impact is that the investment portfolio has been preserved in total relative value.

Remember this *key point* because your strategy is a preservation strategy rather than an accumulation strategy. All of the accumulating has already been done. Now you are preserving the assets or investments relative to all of the risks and relative to the goals and objectives that you have. If you knew with certainty the future, you would not diversify; you would "put all of your eggs in one basket." The best way to prepare for the future and to preserve the investments that you have accumulated is to diversify, diversify, and diversify again.

Very simply, diversification means investing in products in four general areas: liquidity, nonliquidity, growth, and yield. The goal is to diversify or achieve balance between the liquid and nonliquid investments and between the growth and nongrowth investments. For example, a real estate investment is a growth investment that is nonliquid and which guards against inflation and financial risks, but it may take on a business risk, market risk, tax risk, or a legal risk. An investment in a money market fund would eliminate the short-term interest rate risk, but maximize the purchasing power risk and perhaps the financial risk.

The best approach to investment strategy is to design an investment portfolio that will accomplish the universal investment objectives of liquidity, growth, and yield. To meet the risk avoidance objective, measure the whole portfolio by asking yourself, In the event of a market decline, what happens? In the event of a financial collapse, what happens? In the event of business failure, what happens? Analyze the impact of each of these risks upon the entire investment portfolio. Then you need to ask a second question: How likely are these risks to happen? It may be that you are willing to take a risk because your evaluation indicates the risk is very unlikely to occur.

Chart 13–A illustrates the diversification strategy.

There is absolutely no way to avoid all risks, and quite frankly, the number one objective is not necessarily to avoid all the risks. God owns all of my investments and your investments and is in total control of the situation. If I am counting on having a risk-free investment portfolio to give me peace of mind, I will never accomplish it. The Bible has much to say about investments—more about attitude toward handling investments than about how to make investments.

BIBLICAL PRINCIPLES OF INVESTING

1. *Do not presume upon the future.* "Come now, you who say, 'Today or tomorrow we will go to such and such a city, spend a year there, buy and sell, and make a profit'; whereas you do not know what will happen tomorrow. For what is your life? It is even a vapor that appears for a little time and then vanishes away. Instead you ought to say, 'If the Lord wills, we shall live and do this or that'" (James 4:13–15).

2. *Avoid speculation and hasty investment decisions.* "A faithful man will abound with blessings, / But he who hastens to be rich will not go unpunished" (Prov. 28:20). "A man with an evil eye hastens after riches, / And does not consider that poverty will come upon him" (Prov. 28:22). "Dishonest money dwindles away, / but he who gathers money little by little makes it grow" (Prov. 13:11 NIV).

Chart 13–A

DIVERSIFICATION STRATEGY
(PRESERVATION PHASE)

	LIQUID		NON-LIQUID		
Growth	Stocks	$_____	All Real Estate		
	Gold	_____	_____	$_____	
	Silver	_____	_____	_____	
	Other	_____	_____	_____	
	Total	$_____	Total	$_____	= Total Growth Investments $_____
	% of Total	_____%	% of Total	_____%	
Yielding	Cash	_____	Notes Receivable	$_____	
	Savings	_____	Mortgages Receivable	_____	
	Money Market Funds	_____	_____	_____	
	CD's	_____	_____	_____	
	T-Bills	_____	_____	_____	
	Municipal Bonds	_____	_____	_____	
	Total	_____	Total	_____	= Total Yielding Investments $_____
	% of Total	_____%	% of Total	_____%	

Total Liquidity $_____

Key questions after planning the diversification:
1. What is the overall yield? $_____; Percent to total _____%
2. What is a reasonable expectation of overall growth? _____%
3. What is the total liquidity? $_____
4. Is each of the above adequate for my situation? Yes/No _____
5.

	What are the risks?	How likely is the risk to occur?
Business risk	_____	_____%
Financial risk	_____	_____%
Market risk	_____	_____%
Interest rate risk	_____	_____%
Purchasing power risk	_____	_____%
Tax risk	_____	_____%
Legal risk	_____	_____%

3. *Never cosign.* "Do not be one of those who shakes hands in a pledge, / One of those who is surety for debts; / If you have nothing with which to pay, / Why should he take away your bed from under you?" (Prov. 22:26–27). "He who is surety for a stranger will suffer for it, / But one who hates being surety is secure" (Prov. 11:15). "A man devoid of understanding shakes hands in a pledge, / And becomes surety for his friend" (Prov. 17:18).

4. *Evaluate the risk of an investment.* "For which of you, intending to build a tower, does not sit down first and count the cost, whether he has enough to finish it" (Luke 14:28). In other words, is the risk that you are taking worth it? Why are you taking the risk? If the risk does happen, can you afford to lose your investment dollar? Will that change anything for you financially?

5. *Avoid investments that cause anxiety.* "Lord, my heart is not haughty, / Nor my eyes lofty. / Neither do I concern myself with great matters, / Nor with things too profound for me" (Ps. 131:1). "Therefore do not worry, saying, 'What shall we eat?' or 'What shall we drink?' or 'What shall we wear?'" (Matt. 6:31).

6. *Be in unity with your spouse.* Throughout Scripture we are admonished to counsel together and to have a unity in the husband/wife relationship. Often God uses our mates to bring us back to reality. Don't be so foolish or proud as not to take advantage of the partner God has given you.

7. *Avoid high leverage situations.* "The rich rules over the poor, / And the borrower is servant to the lender" (Prov. 22:7).

8. *Avoid deceit.* "The wicked man does deceptive work, / But to him who sows righteousness will be a sure reward" (Prov. 11:18).

9. *Tithe from the current increase rather than the final sale.* Many investors believe that it makes good sense to keep the investment dollars and their increases to make additional investments. Usually the rationale is that they will receive greater tax advantages and be able to multiply these resources even more for the Lord. This rationale is unscriptural because God expects a portion of the increase. "Honor the Lord with your possessions, / And with the firstfruits of all your increase; / So your barns will be filled with plenty, / And your vats will overflow with new wine" (Prov. 3:9–10).

To put off giving under the assumption that the investment will earn more and then you will have more to give is a great danger. This assumption implies that God is *incapable* of using His money today for a greater eternal impact than what I can do by investing.

GENERAL RULES IN SELECTION OF INVESTMENTS

We have discussed common investment mistakes, strategies, tools and techniques, the four investment criteria, risks, diversification and biblical principles. In many ways all investment planning boils down to some very common sense general rules.

1. *Always maintain a long-term perspective.* The longer the term of perspective, the better the decision is apt to be today.

2. *Remember that you can't be an expert on everything.* Be willing to trust others and avoid the pitfall of pride.

3. *High risk to one person is conservative to another.* If a person understands the stock market, stock investments may seem conservative. Another may understand nothing about the stock market, and all stock investments appear to be high risks. An oil and gas investment may be conservative to an oil and gas expert; to the uninitiated in this type of investment, it is almost always a high risk venture.

4. *The personal time required to manage an investment must be considered as a cost.* Many investments, such as stock portfolios, rental property, venture capital, and others, require personal time to ensure that they work out as they are planned. This is a very real cost to the investment, and the benefit, in relation to the cost, must be measured.

5. *Always invest from a strategy.* To do otherwise will always put you in the position of being a responder to investment alternatives as they come along. Knowing what your strategy is and the steps to accomplish this strategy will eliminate almost all investment alternatives that are proposed. Hearing about a "good deal" does not necessarily make it a good deal for you.

6. *Keep it simple.* My general rule is that if you can't explain it to your spouse, then you don't understand it, and you shouldn't do it. If an investment becomes burdensome and seemingly complex, you are probably in an area of investing that you should not be in.

7. *There is no "free lunch."* There is a definite risk/reward relationship—the higher the return you expect, the higher the risk you take. With no exception, a high return will exact a high cost.

8. *Diversify, diversify, diversify.* Never "put all your eggs in one basket." This is the time-tested rule of investing. A friend of mine once told me that the Jewish people in Europe have attempted to preserve their wealth—through centuries of political upheaval—by following three simple rules: Keep it liquid, keep it portable, and keep it diversified.

The summary of what I have said in this chapter is that very few people should be involved in the high-stakes investment game because almost no one has reached the level of Step 6 of the sequential investment strategy. By following the sequential investment strategy you will, by the time of your need, have accomplished almost all of your long-term goals and objectives.

Investing is not difficult, but it certainly can be confusing if you don't keep your priorities straight.

14

Stewardship after Death

YOU MAY HAVE heard about the family who was gathered in the attorney's office eagerly awaiting the reading of the last will and testament of a recently departed family member. It did not take the attorney long to read the very simple will, which merely stated, "Being of sound mind, I spent it all." I have seen bumper stickers in a similar vein, especially near retirement communities, which say, "We're spending our kids' inheritance."

The assumption underlying both quotations is that you can know exactly when and under what circumstances you are going to die. If that is the case, you could plan to have the last penny spent at the moment of death. Unfortunately, the most frequent comment you hear is that "poor John didn't plan on dying so soon" even though "it is appointed for men to die once, but after this the judgment" (Heb. 9:27). Everyone will die; yet very few plan on "dying so soon."

Another reality is found in I Timothy 6:7: "For we brought nothing into this world, and it is certain we can carry nothing out." To paraphrase that verse, "You never see a hearse pulling a U-Haul." John D. Rockefeller's accountant was asked one time, "Can you tell me how much Rockefeller left?" and the accountant said, "Absolutely. Everything."

Our perspective on estate planning is based on these realities: We will all die; we will take nothing with us; and we will probably die at a time other than when we would like. These realities create many practical planning problems.

193

PROBLEMS ASSOCIATED WITH DEATH

The most significant problem associated with death is described in Romans 6:23: "For the wages of sin is death, but the gift of God is eternal life in Christ Jesus our Lord." He who dies without having accepted the gift of Jesus Christ as payment for his own sin is eternally separated from God.

Financial problems are nonexistent in eternity. My prayer is that if any of you reading these words has never accepted the free gift of God's Son as payment for your sins, you would do so and make the most important estate planning step you can ever take. A simple prayer lays the foundation for this estate: "Father, I acknowledge my separation from You, and based upon the death of the Lord Jesus Christ as payment for my sins, I accept the free gift of salvation. Thank You for saving me."

Prior to April of 1974, my life's philosophy could have been summed up by another bumper sticker that you may have seen: "He who dies with the most toys wins." Obviously, that is a delusion because the only one who wins when he dies is the one who has the guarantee of eternal life.

The second problem associated with death is really a set of problems relating to your finances. *Unless you plan the distribution of your estate, the government will.* Your spouse, relatives, or friends are not allowed to plan that distribution—only the owner of assets can plan the distribution through a will. Very rarely does the government have the same objectives for your estate as you do. Additionally, if proper planning has not been done, the final expenses can siphon off up to 70% of an estate. These expenses are for probating the will, estate taxes, inheritance taxes, attorney's fees, accountant's fees, funeral expenses, and the like.

Another financial problem that happens frequently because of poor planning is an estate without enough liquidity to meet the final expenses. Therefore, assets must be sold at depressed values just to generate the cash needed to pay these expenses.

Parents with young children rarely plan to die; yet if they do so without proper planning, the state will determine the guardians for those surviving children. Many times, children also have special needs that call for planning if the parents are not going to be around to handle those needs.

Another problem that is associated with death, or as the life insurance industry puts it, "premature death," is that survivors usually experience handling the details of an estate only once. Consequently, there are few experts and fewer yet who can be explicitly trusted to do things exactly as you would have them to. Therefore, there is a problem of making sure that the administration of the estate is handled as you would have it handled.

ESTATE PLANNING DEFINITIONS

> *Estate Planning is planning for your death so that your family and financial resources are distributed and cared for in accordance with your objectives.*

Distribution. There are only four distribution alternatives available to you: family and friends, charitable organizations, expenses, taxes.

Care. The mental, physical, spiritual, and emotional needs of your family and friends can, to the best of your ability, be planned for in order to minimize their problems.

Financial Resources. Your financial resources consist of your assets, business interests, life insurance, retirement programs, and government benefits programs. These resources are broader in scope than those you include on your net worth statements.

Family. Your immediate family, spiritual family and friends need to be considered in your estate plan.

Objectives. Setting the estate planning objectives is the most difficult part of the estate planning process and can only be accomplished effectively through time and prayer.

A well thought-out estate plan will include not only a will, but also life insurance, correctly owned and with proper beneficiary designations, property deeded appropriately, survivors instructed in both written form and orally as to wishes and desires, proper and easily located records, advisors properly selected and instructed, and perhaps many other things. As can be seen, an estate plan is a very comprehensive plan for death, when planning is no longer possible. Therefore, it must be well-documented and totally complete. Unfortunately, 50% of Americans are estimated not even to have a will, let alone the other elements necessary for a complete and proper estate plan.

REASONS GIVEN FOR NOT PLANNING

"My estate is too small." An estate may be too small to have estate taxes due on it, but there is more to an estate plan than just the tax aspects. Appointing a guardian to care for the children is far too important a matter to be left to a total stranger. In addition, a relatively simple will can avoid many of the administrative costs associated with death.

When considering the size of an estate, many people forget that life insurance can add significantly to an estate size and may cause not only tax problems, but other types of problems as well.

One other reason for planning the estate rather than leaving it for the state court system to handle is that any particular personal effects you want to go to specific relatives or friends must be designated in a will. Otherwise, your intentions mean nothing, and the law of the land will determine who gets what.

"It's too expensive." Many people are "penny-wise and pound-foolish" and think that a will and other actions necessary for proper estate planning are too expensive. First of all, that thought may be an assumption and not a fact. My recommendation is to get an estimate or several estimates from those qualified to prepare the documents. On the other hand probably no price is too great to pay for making it easier on friends and family who have never had to experience life without you.

"I don't have enough time." The underlying reason for this statement is probably a fear of death. Many people superstitiously believe that as long as they don't prepare a will, they won't die. Also, many just avoid talking about death. It is a very uncomfortable topic of discussion for them. Again, with certainty, everyone will die and for the Christian to be superstitious about his or her death is to have a poor understanding of the promises God has made in the Bible.

"I'm not certain about what I want to do." Because estate planning can be a very complex and certainly unfamiliar topic, many do not know how to go about setting those objectives. This is a legitimate concern. However, God promises to provide us the wisdom that we need (see James 1:5), and when we are planning for the future, we need God's wisdom for certain.

Second, no estate plan needs to be written in concrete. The design should always be flexible since our needs, desires, and circumstances change over time.

In this chapter I will outline the objectives that you need to consider in designing an estate plan. I will introduce the very technical areas of estate planning, but I also recommend that everyone see an attorney or accountant, at least every other year, to develop or review an estate plan. Estate planning may very well require input from many professionals such as a tax attorney, life insurance agent, bank trust officer, financial planner, and friends and family. I simply want to get you started in the process.

ESTATE PLANNING OBJECTIVES

Distribution of Financial Resources

There are only four alternatives available for the allocation of your financial resources: family and friends, charity, taxes, and expenses. You should plan this allocation after spending time with God so as to minimize the shrinkage from unnecessary expenses. The potential for conflict is great when it comes to predetermining priorities. My challenge to the people that I work with is to list these four alternatives and then to put either a percent or a dollar amount next to each one in order to quantify how they want their estate distributed. Generally speaking, if you can quantify where you want your estate ultimately to end up, then the estate plan can be drafted accordingly. The problem is that most people do not know or will not decide how they want their estate to be allocated.

Obviously, within the categories of family and friends and charity, there can be many alternatives.

Provide Estate Liquidity

Liquidity always provides flexibility. If an estate has any size at all, flexibility is needed to provide for the transition period immediately after one's death until assets can be transferred, retitled, and released. In addition, liquidity helps prevent the sale of nonliquid assets in perhaps an unfavorable economic environment when they would lose their true value. Liquidity is also needed to pay taxes, if any are due, and liquidity makes it easier to distribute an estate among several beneficiaries.

One of the most nonliquid assets that can typically have significant size is the value in a closely held business. By planning for the proper amount of liquidity, a closely held business can continue to function and provide the security needed for both the employees and owners. Insufficient liquidity can force the sale of a business at perhaps an inopportune time.

Provide for Ease of Management and Administration of Estate

Many times a wife is left after the death of her husband with no experience in managing assets. She undoubtedly would have the ability to do so with proper training, but suddenly she is overwhelmed with the responsibility for more money than she has ever imagined from life insurance and other assets. However, to select an executor or trustee other than a spouse may mean that control for the management and administration of the estate passes to a nonfamily member.

The person doing the estate planning must provide for the administration and management of the estate, taking into account the experience and ability of those appointed to this role. My advice is typically to name the spouse as executor and trustee because he or she can always hire any counsel that is needed to manage the estate's assets properly. When control is given to a corporate entity, such as a bank or a nonfamily member then control literally passes at the point of death, and that too often becomes a poor stewardship decision in retrospect. Story after story can be told of widows at the mercy of nonsympathetic former business partners, bank trust officers, family friends, or even other family members.

I recommend that all parties affected by an estate plan review it together so their responsibilities can be clearly delineated by the one who is leaving the estate. While there is still opportunity, the individual should articulate his or her desires in front of all the family members and friends who are impacted. Admittedly, this is something that is very, very rarely done—it never seems important until it is too late!

I always recommend that a husband honor the absolute obligation to train his wife to manage whatever God has entrusted to the two of them. Otherwise, she has been effectively disinherited.

I remember visiting with a man who wanted me to help him plan his estate. He literally had several million dollars in cash which constituted his entire estate. He had no debts, a great marriage, and a desire to leave his estate ultimately to the Lord's work. As we were discussing the estate plan, he advised me that his wife had no idea how much they were worth. She trusted him implicitly with their financial situation and never questioned his decisions. However, when he described his intentions of giving away his entire estate, I asked him how his wife was going to feel when the will was read and she realized that she had had no part in determining where the millions were to go. They had several children, all of whom were at that time doing well spiritually and financially, but circumstances could change and his wife would have no opportunity to provide for any of the children or grandchildren under the proposed estate plan.

When I confronted him with his wife's potential feelings, he immediately saw the error in his thinking, went home and shared his plans with his wife. Together they developed an estate plan that provided a bit more flexibility for her, but still accomplished the objectives he had for the ultimate distribution of the estate. That could have been a very tragic story had the man not included his wife in determining the objectives for the estate.

Provide for Care of Immediate Family

When children are young, guardianship in the event of the death of both parents must be addressed. Also, the education needs, the physical needs, and the mental or emotional needs, of children may change with time. For example, a proper estate plan must be in place for a physically or mentally handicapped child. Older persons may plan to provide for the special needs of their grandchildren.

Provide for the care of the family also means that you have as an objective to maintain the lifestyle of the surviving spouse for some time period.

Provide for Grown Children

There is a fine line between provision and protection. We are to provide for our families, but not to the extent that they have no opportunity to trust God for work in their lives. Many children—and even young adults—have been ruined by overindulgent parents who left everything to them without considering the ramifications of doing this in their children's lives.

It is a parent's responsibility, according to Proverbs 22:6, to "train up a child in the way he should go." That responsibility does not end when the child leaves home, and if the parents have failed in the training, then I suggest that they not compound that failure by leaving financial resources that protect the children from God's dealing with them in their adult lives.

I also believe that a parent should recognize differences in children—differences due to age, temperament, their demonstrated ability to handle money, their spiritual commitment, their spiritual maturity, their known or unknown marriage partners, and their children. It is a parent and grandparent's responsibility to entrust God's resources to children only if they have demonstrated the ability to handle those resources in a manner that would be pleasing to Him who is the owner of all.

If a parent entrusts God's resources to a slothful child, it is no different than giving those resources to any slothful stranger. Just because you have a child does not make the child the automatic beneficiary of your estate. I believe that more prayer, wisdom, and decisiveness are needed in meeting this objective of providing for grown children than any other estate planning area. Obviously, great emotion and perhaps tradition are involved.

Provide for Charity

Unless you plan for charitable giving in your estate plan, it won't happen. Because any charitable gifts given at death are a deduction from the total estate for estate tax purposes, all charitable giving at death reduces the estate taxes payable. The trade-off almost always becomes one between giving to family members and giving to charity and is never an easy question to handle. My own belief is that the majority of charitable giving should be done while the income is being earned rather than delayed until death. After death, you have no more control over the property anyway, and it is not actually giving in the sense of giving up anything. I also believe that giving at death is an opportunity to continue having an impact for Christ on earth while you are enjoying your new relationship with Him in heaven.

One means for your estate to continue to give to charity after your death is through a charitable trust described later in this chapter.

Provide Testimony

My mother-in-law died recently. Along with her will was a note to her children that her greatest desire was for them to accept Jesus Christ as their personal Savior and to spend eternity with her. She was sure of her relationship with Him. A will can provide a public record of your Christian testimony, not only for your children but also for anyone else who reads that document, including attorneys, judges, accountants, and perhaps grandchildren, great-grandchildren, and the like. Obviously, without a will, you do not have that public testimony.

Provide for Future Planning Flexibility

Because circumstances and desires change over time, very little of an estate plan should be "written in concrete." In other words, irrevocable decisions need to be postponed, if possible, until death. The typical estate plan does not come into being until death. However, when an estate gets to be fairly sizeable, certain irrevocable decisions, such as property ownership, may have to be made. My recommendation is that all such decisions be made only when absolutely necessary and beneficial.

TYPES OF PROPERTY

In reviewing Figure 14.1 on page 202, you see there are basically four kinds of property for estate planning purposes and that these four types of property will pass through an estate at death in one of three ways—by will, by contract, or by law. Proper estate planning calls for coordinating the types of property so as to minimize the amount that passes out the spigot for taxes and expenses, thereby allowing the maximum amount to flow directly to the family and charity.

To illustrate the complexity of coordinating agreements, contracts, and law, let's assume a situation in which by will a husband leaves everything to his wife and children, including their vacation home. However, the vacation home is owned jointly by the husband and his brother, having been passed to them by their parents. If the property deed is a joint tenancy deed, it means that the surviving tenant will succeed to ownership of the property. Therefore, when the husband died, the brother owned 100% of the vacation home, even though the husband's will specified that the property was to go to the children.

Potentially more devastating is the death of a man who owns his own business in partnership with a nonfamily member and there is no buy/ sell agreement. A woman can be left with ownership in the business, but no means of obtaining a fair price from the partners. In addition, they may refuse to pay her any type of dividend or income from the business, so she is effectively cut off from all income.

Figure 14.1

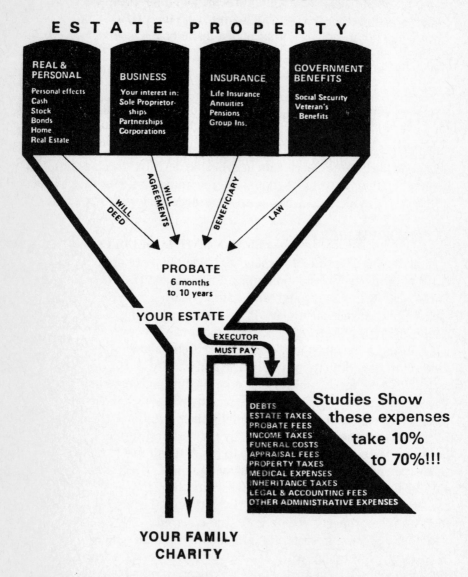

PROPERTY DILUTION ILLUSTRATION

ESTATE PROPERTY

REAL & PERSONAL

Personal effects
Cash
Stock
Bonds
Home
Real Estate

BUSINESS

Your interest in:
Sole Proprietor-
ships
Partnerships
Corporations

INSURANCE

Life Insurance
Annuities
Pensions
Group Ins.

GOVERNMENT BENEFITS

Social Security
Veteran's
Benefits

WILL
DEED

WILL
AGREEMENTS

BENEFICIARY

LAW

PROBATE
6 months
to 10 years

YOUR ESTATE

EXECUTOR
MUST PAY

DEBTS
ESTATE TAXES
PROBATE FEES
INCOME TAXES
FUNERAL COSTS
APPRAISAL FEES
PROPERTY TAXES
MEDICAL EXPENSES
INHERITANCE TAXES
LEGAL & ACCOUNTING FEES
OTHER ADMINISTRATIVE EXPENSES

Studies Show
these expenses
take 10%
to 70%!!!

YOUR FAMILY CHARITY

For relatively simple estates consisting of homes, personal property, and perhaps a few investments, it is not difficult to coordinate your will, all contracts, and the law in order to accomplish the desired results in an estate plan; but it certainly should be reviewed by a competent professional to ensure that the desired results will take place.

ESTATE TAXES

The only two certainties in life are taxes and death. Under current estate tax law, it *is* possible not to have any taxes due at death, but the ultimate objective in estate planning is not necessarily to eliminate all taxes. To understand this statement, you need to understand some things about the following elements of estate taxes:

Chart 14–A

UNIFIED TRANSFER TAX RATE SCHEDULES

If the amount is:		Tentative tax is:			
Over	But not over	Tax	+	%	On Excess Over
0	$ 10,000	0	18		0
$ 10,000	20,000	$ 1,800	20		$ 10,000
20,000	40,000	3,800	22		20,000
40,000	60,000	8,200	24		40,000
60,000	80,000	13,000	26		60,000
80,000	100,000	18,200	28		80,000
100,000	150,000	23,800	30		100,000
150,000	250,000	38,800	32		150,000
250,000	500,000	70,800	34		250,000
500,000	750,000	155,800	37		500,000
750,000	1,000,000	248,300	39		750,000
1,000,000	1,250,000	345,800	41		1,000,000
1,250,000	1,500,000	448,300	43		1,250,000
1,500,000	2,000,000	555,800	45		1,500,000
2,000,000	2,500,000	780,800	49		2,000,000
2,500,000		1,025,800	50		2,500,000

- Uniform federal estate and gift tax rates
- Annual gift tax exclusion
- Marital deduction
- Unified credit
- Marital gift exclusion

Uniform Federal Estate and Gift Tax Rates

In Chart 14.1 you see a tax table that is used to calculate what are commonly known as transfer taxes. Property is transferred when a person dies, or prior to death if the property is a gift to noncharitable organizations or persons. In each case the transfer of that property is taxed. The theory behind that tax is that the original owner no longer controls that property and the government has a right to tax transfers of property just as it has a right to tax income, sales, or whatever else it chooses to tax. Estate taxes used to be eliminated or avoided by transferring property prior to death because tax rates were less for the gifting of property than they were for the transfer upon death. However, Congress unified the estate and gift tax rates to make them the same no matter when the property is transferred. The tax imposed will be at the rates indicated in Chart 14–A.

Property transferred to charitable organizations, either prior to death or at death, escapes all transfer taxes. If the objective is to pay no taxes, that is possible by either giving away all property prior to death to a charitable organization or passing the property to charitable organizations at death. This is why I said that it is possible to avoid paying estate taxes but not in every case is it wise to do so. It is also possible to transfer property with no taxes due *prior* to death by means of what is called the annual gift exclusion or marital gift exclusion and *at* death by use of the marital deduction.

Annual Gift Exclusion

On Chart 14–A, you will note that a gift of up to $10,000 can be made to a noncharitable organization with no tax being due. In reality, any one person can give away any number of $10,000 gifts to any number of persons with no transfer tax being imposed. Therefore, a husband and wife together could give to each of their children $20,000 per year—an annual gift exclusion. As a matter of fact, they can give to other individuals whether or not they are related to them.

This can be a very beneficial way to transfer property with no tax. I point out, though, that this property does not qualify for a charitable deduction on the income tax return—only gifts to charitable organizations qualify for such a deduction.

In estate planning, it is frequently advantageous for parents to begin a "gifting" program to their children of property that is likely to appreciate in value, thereby each year transferring property to them and removing it from the parents' estate, not only at its current value but at its appreciated value which will be taxed at a higher rate. For example, if a parent transfers to a child $10,000 worth of stock that ultimately appreciates to $100,000, he would have effectively removed $100,000 from being taxed had he waited until death to transfer that property.

For an illustration of how this can work in fairly large numbers, assume a couple has three children, all of whom are married and each of whom have two children. The three children plus three spouses plus six more children make a total of twelve family members. Because both the husband and wife can each give $10,000 to each family member, potentially they can give $240,000 every year to their family—$10,000 from each parent to each child, spouse, and grandchild.

Marital Gift Exclusion

In addition to the annual gift exclusion, one spouse may transfer to another spouse prior to death an unlimited amount of property and not be subject to a transfer tax. Even if one had an estate of $100,000,000, it could be transferred to the spouse free of taxes prior to death.

One of the reasons why this provision may be used is to take full advantage of the "unified credit," as explained below. Another reason for removing property from one spouse is to protect that property in the event of a lawsuit. For example, a physician who has the risk of a malpractice suit could transfer the family residence to his/her spouse to protect it from being taken.

Marital Deduction

Even if a spouse does not transfer property prior to death, an unlimited transfer with no estate taxes occurs at death through what is called the marital deduction. Regardless of the size of the estate, there are no transfer taxes imposed if the estate is left to the spouse who is still living. There is a problem when the surviving spouse dies in that he or she presumably has no spouse to leave the property to; it is all subject to taxes with two exceptions—property left to charity and an amount known as the unified credit amount.

Unified Credit

Under the Economic Recovery Tax Act of 1981 a credit of $192,800 is allowed beginning in 1987 (for 1986, this amount is $155,800). Referring to Chart 14–A, you see that if an estate, after expenses and charitable contributions are taken out, has $600,000 subject to tax, the tax on that $600,000 is $192,800. Strictly by law, a credit is allowed for the first $192,800 of taxes due. Therefore, if the calculated estate tax is $192,800 or less, there is effectively no tax due on an estate.

Even if $600,000 of property is transferred prior to death and both the annual gift tax exclusion and the marital gift exclusion have been used, there is a credit against the transfer tax of $192,800 due on that transfer. No tax is due on that transfer. Prior to death or at death, all credits that have been used cannot be greater than $192,800. In other words, you only get to use the total credit once—not prior to death and again at death.

Because of the current law provisions allowing for the marital deduction, annual gift exclusion, and unified credit, it is possible to have an estate of up to $1,200,000 and pay no estate taxes. This is true because both a husband and wife are entitled to the unified credit. Therefore, a husband can have an estate subject to taxation of $600,000 and pay no taxes and a wife can have an estate of $600,000 and pay no taxes. Obviously, each spouse needs to have no more than $600,000 in his or her name at death if the objective is to pay no taxes.

Ultimately, the only way to avoid paying transfer taxes is to transfer property prior to death using the annual gift exclusion to family members, or prior to death, to give it to charitable organizations, or at death to give it to charitable organizations so that the total estate is no more than $600,000 per person. The point is, this all requires planning, and one of the planning tools that must be used is a will.

WILLS

A will is a written, witnessed document that defines your final wishes and desires regarding many things, including property distribution. A person who dies with a will is called one who dies testate. A person who dies without a will, dies intestate, and the laws of intestacy apply.

The laws of intestacy differ from state to state, but in general, if one dies intestate, that person gives the state government the right to determine:

- The control of their financial resources
- The distribution of those resources
- The choice of executor
- The choice of a guardian for minor children
- The ability to waive fiduciary bonds
- The right to authorize a business continuation plan

On the other hand, a person who dies with a will retains the following:

- The control of the use of their assets
- The distribution of those assets
- The bequeathing of specific personal possessions to loved ones
- The choice of the executor
- The choice of a guardian for minor children
- The right to waive fiduciary bonds (such bonds can be expensive)
- The right to set up various trusts to reduce estate taxes and probate costs

There are basically three kinds of wills: the "I Love You" will, the A-B Trust will, and pour-over wills.

"I Love You" Will

This is commonly known as a "simple will" which basically leaves everything to the surviving spouse. If a total estate is under $600,000 in size, there are no taxes at the death of the first spouse to die and no taxes at the second to die. However, if the second spouse to die lives very long after the first one dies, there can be substantial appreciation in property values, thus negating the tax planning that was done in that type of will. This is another reason why estate planning should be reviewed on a frequent basis. Obviously, if an estate is greater than $600,000 in size, there can be substantial taxes when the second spouse dies, even though there is no tax when the first dies. This is the reason that another type of will is more commonly used today in estates of $600,000 or greater.

A-B Trust Will

This type of will is illustrated in Figure 14.2 and provides for a gross estate to be divided into two shares at the death of the first spouse to die. An A share goes into what is called "a marital trust," and a B share goes into what is called "a residual trust." The marital trust is totally controlled and owned by the surviving spouse, who has all of the rights to that property. It will be included in the surviving spouse's gross estate, and if the amount left in the marital trust is greater than $600,000, there will be taxes paid at the survivor's subsequent death.

The residual trust is left with certain rights given to the surviving spouse, but the ultimate ownership of the property remains in trust until the survivor dies, and then the property goes directly to the children or other heirs. From a tax planning standpoint, the objective is to put up to $600,000 of the gross estate into the residual trust. The property that goes into the residual trust is fully taxable when the first spouse dies, but the unified credit of $192,800 offsets the tax on the transferred property.

If the total estate after debts and expenses is $1,200,000 at the first to die, then $600,000 is put into the residual trust. This means that there is no tax paid on that amount, and the other $600,000 is put into the marital trust, which at the survivor's death means there is no tax paid on that amount. The children or other heirs are thus able to receive $1,200,000 with no estate taxes being paid on the estate. Obviously, most Americans may use either a simple will or an A-B trust will to eliminate any estate taxes that might come due upon the death of both the husband and the wife.

Pour-over wills

A pour-over will simply leaves everything of the first to die to a revocable living trust that has already been set up. The revocable living trust then provides for the formation of the two A-B trusts just described. To understand the benefit of this method it is necessary to understand some simple concepts regarding trusts.

Figure 14.2

THE A-B TRUST WILL

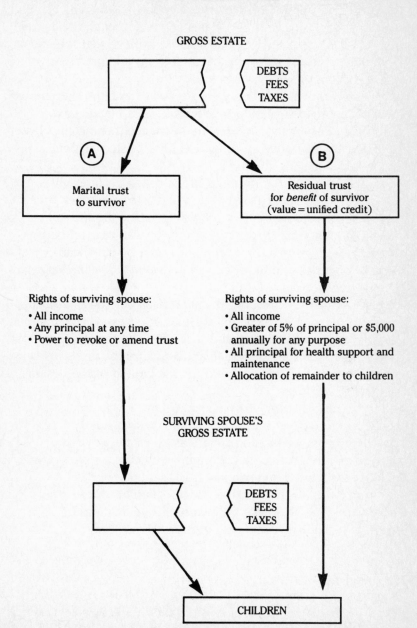

GROSS ESTATE

DEBTS
FEES
TAXES

A

Marital trust
to survivor

B

Residual trust
for *benefit* of survivor
(value = unified credit)

Rights of surviving spouse:

• All income
• Any principal at any time
• Power to revoke or amend trust

Rights of surviving spouse:

• All income
• Greater of 5% of principal or $5,000
  annually for any purpose
• All principal for health support and
  maintenance
• Allocation of remainder to children

SURVIVING SPOUSE'S
GROSS ESTATE

DEBTS
FEES
TAXES

CHILDREN

TRUSTS

A trust is simply a separate taxable entity that is generally set up by an attorney or through a will. A trust per se will not reduce taxes, but its use may aid in tax reduction. Many persons believe that the use of a trust automatically reduces taxes, but it doesn't; it is merely a vehicle that may aid in the reduction of taxes.

A trust involves three parties: (1) a trustor or grantor, the one who sets the trust up and transfers property to it; (2) a beneficiary, the one who receives some beneficial interest in the trust, either income or property, or both, at some point in time; and (3) a trustee, the one who is responsible for managing the trust.

A trust that is set up during one's life is called an inter-vivos trust, whereas one that is set up at death is called a testamentary trust. An inter-vivos trust can have two characteristics. It can either be revocable—meaning that the trustor or grantor can revoke the trust at any time and take the property back—or it can be irrevocable, which means that the trustor or grantor cannot in any way take back property once it has been transferred to a trust.

Persons generally use trusts to manage assets for those who are incompetent to manage or incapable of managing assets: for example, handicapped children, elderly, young children. The trustee, then, takes the place of that incompetent person and manages the assets in accordance with the terms of the trust and for the benefit of the designated parties to the trust.

The second reason to use a trust is to avoid most probate costs. Unlike an individual, a trust does not die. If an individual's property is held by a trust, the trust is not subject to probate as an estate would be.

Third, trusts are used as tax planning vehicles, as previously described, with the marital and residual trusts set up under an A-B will. In addition to those trusts that are used for tax planning, there are various charitable trusts that also have tax planning ramifications.

Lastly, there is an irrevocable life insurance trust that can also be set up for tax planning purposes.

Revocable Living Trust

A revocable living trust is a trust set up during the life of the grantor that can be used to manage the person's assets in the event that he or she ultimately becomes incapable of managing them for mental or physical reasons. Then, at death the trust becomes a vehicle for all the property that is then transferred to a marital or residual trust. The pour-over will described previously pours all of the assets of an estate into a previously established revocable living trust and then out of that living trust into the marital or residual trust. This type of trust can be especially beneficial for accomplishing management goals and tax planning goals, but it is most beneficial for accomplishing the goal of reducing estate expenses—specifically probate expenses. A revocable living trust avoids many of the attorney, accountant, and court costs associated with estate administration. This trust also provides privacy with regard to the distribution of estate assets because there is no court record made of those assets and their distribution.

Marital Deduction Trust

A marital deduction trust is a trust that is the recipient of property at the death of a first spouse that provides for the management of the assets by a trustee (who can be, in this case, also the beneficiary of the trust, the surviving spouse). The primary requirement of a marital trust is that all of the income must go exclusively to the surviving spouse for use as he or she sees fit.

The trustor or grantor is the first spouse to die, the beneficiary is the surviving spouse, and the trustee can be either the surviving spouse or anyone else selected by the grantor.

I typically recommend that the surviving spouse be the trustee as well as the beneficiary so that he or she has the total control over those assets. The possibility exists, of course, that the surviving spouse may be incapable of managing the assets.

Residual Trust

A residual trust is sometimes called a by-pass trust—meaning that it by-passes the estate of the surviving spouse. In this case the grantor (the first to die) has two beneficiaries, an income beneficiary, who is the surviving spouse, and a residual beneficiary, who is the children or other heirs. The trustee can be the surviving spouse but does not have to be, and there are good reasons for having a third party trustee when there may be a conflict within a family.

Charitable Trusts

Property transferred into a trust by a grantor has two types of on-going characteristics or benefits—one is an *income benefit* and the other is a *remainder benefit*. The beneficiaries can be divided so that one beneficiary receives the income and the other beneficiary receives the remainder interest. If one of the beneficiaries is a charitable organization, then there is a tax benefit that falls to the grantor from having set up this kind of trust.

This tax benefit is actuarially determined, depending upon the age of the grantor and the length of time until the benefit is received, thereby creating either an income tax deduction or an estate tax deduction, or in some cases, both deductions, depending upon all of these factors.

A charitable lead trust basically gives the income benefit to a charitable organization, but the remainder interest goes to someone else. A charitable lead trust, if it is a testamentary trust, can qualify for an estate tax deduction. The amount of the deduction is actuarially determined, but the trust is a way for those with charitable inclinations to give away an income interest in property, but retain the property for the use of children or grandchildren.

A charitable remainder trust, on the other hand, retains the income for someone but gives the remainder interest to charity. It also can be set up while both spouses are living or at the death of one and, again, can qualify for either an income tax deduction or an estate tax deduction or both. One of the primary uses of this type of trust is to receive property that is generating an income while retaining the income right to that property so that upon the death of the first or second to die the remainder interest goes into charity. This insures an income stream, but it also provides for no estate tax on that property since it will pass to a charity upon death. Whether or not it provides a current income tax deduction depends upon an actuarially computed percent.

Both of these types of trusts, charitable lead trusts and charitable remainder trusts, are very effective tools for estate planning, but they are also quite complex and should not be set up without considering the estate plan in its entirety. If these potentially apply to you, I recommend, without question, that you contact an attorney and perhaps even the charitable organization that could be a beneficiary to assist you in evaluating the applicability and implementation of these trusts.

Irrevocable Life Insurance Trust

One other type of estate planning trust is the irrevocable life insurance trust. An irrevocable life insurance trust is, as its name implies, irrevocable and it holds, as an owner, life insurance policies. Life insurance proceeds are normally not taxable unless the owner, insured, and beneficiary are the same. This circumstance can happen if the wife dies first and leaves everything to her husband. An irrevocable life insurance trust can avoid this kind of tax problem.

This trust is also a fairly sophisticated estate planning tool because of the gift and income tax consequences in setting it up and maintaining it. Once again, professional help and consideration of all the other estate planning objectives are called for.

In summary, trusts will not reduce estate taxes by themselves—rather the transfer of property reduces estate taxes. Trusts are merely vehicles, and when one uses a trust the ownership has been transferred either for a temporary time period or perhaps permanently. When you hear others talking about the use of trusts to reduce estate taxes, keep in mind that a trust is not a panacea for every estate planning problem. Used properly, it can be an effective tool for effective estate planning. The general rule to follow is that there is always some cost associated with anything that appears to provide a benefit—in other words, there is "no free lunch."

LIFE INSURANCE

A classic example of there being no free lunch is life insurance. It seems so easy to create a million dollar estate through the purchase of life insurance. However, the cost is two-fold—paying the premiums while living and having to die to collect the benefits. Life insurance is in reality nothing more than a tool to be used in estate planning.

Life insurance can be used in basically three ways in estate planning: first of all, to create an estate for younger families; second, to provide the necessary liquidity to pay for taxes, death expenses, and to fund business buy/sell agreements; and third, to provide charitable giving dollars that are not otherwise available. In other words, life insurance is purchased with a specific objective in mind rather than just because someone else has it.

I am asked many times to give the biblical perspective on life insurance. Is it a lack of faith to purchase life insurance? In our society, my judgment is that I Timothy 5:8 is really the controlling verse, and that verse requires a father to provide for his family. If his church, or other members of his family do not have the desire or ability to provide for a young family, then without question I believe it is poor stewardship not to have enough life insurance.

Life insurance, however, does not eliminate the responsibility of the church to care for its own. Unfortunately, as we have become more mobile in our society and have fewer close relationships, the church itself does not feel the burden of caring for those in its midst who have a legitimate need. Therefore, I do believe life insurance should be used as an estate planning tool. I also see nothing in the Scriptures against using life insurance to provide liquidity or to meet charitable giving objectives. In other words, it is still a matter of provision or protection. If life insurance is a provision to meet certain objectives, it is certainly all right to have it. However, if life insurance is a substitute for God's protection in my life, it is not right.

CHARITABLE GIVING

I want to conclude this lengthy chapter with a reminder that the only sure way to reduce estate taxes is to transfer property. At death, the only deduction given for the transfer of property is for that property to be transferred to a qualifying charitable organization. Charitable giving as a part of the estate plan should certainly be considered in light of the total income tax objectives.

Charitable giving should not be done, however, as an attempt to repay God for His blessings to you during your life, because as I have said frequently, giving at death does not result in a reward for the Christian. You have no choice at death. You leave it all here anyway.

Nor should charitable giving be done at death when it may threaten the well-being of the surviving spouse and family. That, to me, is a higher priority and specifically commanded in the Scriptures (see I Timothy 5:8).

Charitable giving certainly fits in most estate plans. Let me recommend a book entitled *Leave Your House in Order* by John G. Watts for a much more extensive analysis of estate planning, especially from a biblical and charitable perspective.

Estate planning is an integral part of financial planning, but it is not financial planning in its entirety. Both financial planning and estate planning need to begin at an early age. They are dynamic in nature and to procrastinate in either area is poor stewardship.

15

Faith or Foolishness

SEVERAL YEARS AGO a speaker at a missions conference in my church quoted the statistics that show more money is spent on both chewing gum and dog food in the United States than is given to foreign missions. I cannot vouch for the accuracy of these numbers, but I do not doubt them. I do know the IRS reports that Americans, on the average, give less than 1.7% of their adjusted gross income for charitable contributions.

As a financial planner, my first paying client was a man who said his goal for the rest of his life was to retire just as soon as possible in order to work full time on the mission field. In addition, he wanted to maintain his present lifestyle and continue to give at the 15% level as he was then doing. He was a fifty-two-year-old physician with two children who were both educated. He had a net worth of around $350,000, and his income was approximately $85,000 per year. I asked him and his wife to share with me any dreams they might have for their lives. They both agreed that one of their desires was to give $1,000,000 to the Lord's work before they died. I thought to myself that this was obviously impossible with their income and net worth.

However, about 60 days later after their financial plan was prepared, I called him and said, "Doc, I hope you're sitting down, because I have some shocking news for you. First of all, how would you like to retire in five years and have approximately $1,000,000 in investments at that time?" He thought that sounded like a great idea, and then I told him that, according to our projections, it was also possible for them to give away $1,000,000 during that same five-year time period. To say the least, he was shocked and frankly disbelieving.

I met with him and his wife to go over their plan and showed them that they, in fact, had a much higher net worth than they originally thought because of the escalation in value of some of the real estate they owned. By taking a long-range perspective on their planning, it was possible for them to begin giving away some of their assets while they were, at the same time, replacing them out of their current cash flow. Finally, I told them that all of this was possible for two reasons: first of all, because of their desire to give, and second, because they had lived, and were continuing to live, a nonconsumptive lifestyle.

It has now been several years since we prepared their plan. Even though it did not work out exactly as projected, they have been fairly well able to accomplish the objectives they originally gave me . . . because God always has creative alternatives.

I have been able to share the same principles that I learned from this couple with others, and we have seen many clients make a commitment to give substantial sums of money. From my observations I think there are three reasons why Christians, who desire to give, don't give more.

First of all, they don't know that they can give and still meet the other goals and objectives they have. They have never really gathered together an analysis of all their financial resources to know what obligations and opportunities they have. It is very difficult to be a good steward when you don't know what you have.

Second, they don't know how to give. They are not aware of all the various ways to give. In the doctor's case, one of the techniques that we used was to give away property that had appreciated in value, thereby avoiding the capital gains tax on it. Furthermore, he still got a deduction for the full fair market value of the property. Through the use of this technique, he was able to reduce his taxes to a very low amount, which thus freed up cash to be invested in replacement of the property that had been given. It still cost him to do the giving, but it cost him less to give this way than if he had given cash.

The third and most important reason that people don't give is that they don't *plan* to give. It is the same issue that we have been dealing with throughout this book: We live a life of being a responder rather than a planner. In working with our clients, it has been my experience that, with planning, their giving goes up, on an average, about four times what they were giving prior to doing planning. A very well-known and wealthy American told me one time, "Any man, and especially a businessman, has more uses for money than the money available.

Therefore, unless he plans to give, he never will give." A person whose lifestyle is consumptive can never accumulate enough to be able to give substantial amounts of money away. Giving is never a cause of spiritual growth—it is rather a function of spiritual growth.

BIBLICAL ANSWERS TO THE QUESTIONS OF GIVING

There are three very relevant questions you should ask yourself as you plan to give:

1. When should I give?
2. Where should I give?
3. How much should I give?

As a result of reviewing guidelines and principles in the Scripture, I believe there are six words that answer the questions, when to give, where to give, and how much to give:

1. When?
   • Preemptively
   • Periodically
2. Where?
   • Purposefully
3. How much?
   • Proportionately
   • Planned
   • Precommitted

When to Give

Preemptive giving is clearly defined in Proverbs 3:9: "Honor the Lord with your possessions, / And with the firstfruits of all your increase." To me, this means that giving should have the first priority over all other uses of money, and therefore I give, preempting all other uses, until I have met that commitment.

"On the first day of the week let each one of you lay something aside, storing up as he may prosper, that there be no collections when I come" (I Cor. 16:2). Not only should I give preemptively, but I should also give periodically. To take this Scripture literally would be to say that, on each

Sunday of the week, some amount should be put aside and saved for giving purposes. So the "when" question is answered—giving should be the first priority use of the income, and this giving should be done as it is received, that is, on a periodic basis.

Where to Give

When answering the question, Where should I give? we should make a purposeful decision to give where the Scripture says God's interest is. "For the administration of this service not only supplies the needs of the saints, but also is abounding through many thanksgivings to God" (II Cor. 9:12).

God definitely commands us to meet the needs of the saints and to fulfill the Great Commission. Thus, our purposes in giving are to give for the needy, for evangelism, and for discipleship in *our* Judea, *our* Samaria, and to the uttermost parts of the earth (see Acts 1:8). Giving must be taken very seriously and decided upon consciously in order to fulfill the commands of Scripture.

To help answer the question, Where should I give? we can build a matrix. Down one side are the biblical admonitions to give to evangelism, discipleship, the poor, the widows, the orphans, and the needy. Across the top of the chart are the locations—Judea, Samaria, and the uttermost parts of the earth, or in our contemporary situations, the city, the state, the United States, and the rest of the world.

As you review this chart, write in the giving that you are now doing. You will be able to see how well you are fulfilling the biblical admonitions in terms of places and needs. You then need to ask the question, Am I giving all that I should be giving?

How Much to Give

How much to give in quantitative terms is not as important as our attitude toward giving. In II Corinthians 9:7 we read that our giving should be done "not grudgingly or of necessity; for God loves a cheerful giver." In II Corinthians 8:9, Paul gave us the example of Christ to suggest the right attitude toward giving: "For you know the grace of our Lord Jesus Christ, that though He was rich, yet for your sakes He became poor, that you through His poverty might become rich." So, the attitude of giving must be one of cheerfulness and grace. Freely we have received, freely we must give.

Chart 15-A

GIVING PLAN

WHERE (Geographically)

WHERE (Activities)	MY CITY	MY STATE	MY COUNTRY	WORLD	HOW MUCH (1)
EVANGELISM					
DISCIPLESHIP					
POOR					
WIDOWS					
ORPHANS					
TOTAL	$				TOTAL $

(1) How much:
    Proportionately—should _____
    Planned—could _____
    Precommitted—would _____
    TOTAL $_____

When:
    As received—Preemptively
               —Periodically

The question, How much should I give? is not a simple matter. "For I bear witness that according to their ability, yes, and beyond their ability, they were freely willing, imploring us with much urgency that we would receive the gift and the fellowship of the ministering to the saints. And this they did, not as we had hoped, but first gave themselves to the Lord, and then to us by the will of God" (2 Cor. 8:3–5). Therefore, we are not limited in how much we give either by what we can see or according to our abilities.

Through consideration of the three P's we have mentioned we can come to a right answer of how much: we should give *proportionately* on a *planned* basis, and on a *precommitted* basis. Give an amount that is proportionate to the amount that God has prospered you. You should, by planning, give more than a proportionate amount, and you should pre-commit to give some of the amount God provides on a totally unexpected basis.

APPLICATION

These principles work themselves out in three levels of giving—the "should give" level, the "could give" level, and the "would give" level. The "should give" level includes our proportionate giving. Each Christian should give in proportion to the amount that he or she has received.

The "could give" level is the amount that I could give if I were willing to give up something else. It may mean that I give up a vacation, a savings account, a lifestyle desire, or something else. Giving at this level is the closest any American Christian can come to sacrificial giving as described in Luke 21:4: "for all these out of their abundance have put in offerings for God, but she out of her poverty has put in all the livelihood that she had." Sacrificial giving is giving up something in order to give to the Lord. I recommend that after a financial plan is put together a family should regularly choose to give up something in order to give at the could give level. This level requires no faith, so it is not a faith pledge. There is no faith required because you can see the amount, and faith, by definition, requires seeing the unseen.

The third level of giving more clearly approximates faith giving, and I call it the precommitted giving or the "would give" level. We commit ourselves to giving if God provides a certain amount supernaturally. God can do this only if there is a financial plan in place that allows us to see His providing an additional cash flow margin through either additional income or decreased expense. Unless we are precommitted to give the additional surplus, we will not give it.

In summary, how much we can give is dependent upon three levels: I should give an amount proportionate to my income; I could give an additional amount by giving up something; and I would give more if God increased my cash flow margin. The how much is not dependent upon a set formula, and it gives us the opportunity to see God at work in our financial lives.

Many times I am asked whether one should give now or should build an investment base in order to be able to give late. In our earlier illustrations, we saw that $10,000 compounding at 25% over 40 years grows to $75,231,000. Wouldn't a person do better to find an investment at 25% to compound it and then give the $75,231,000 rather than the mere $10,000?

The way I answer this question is with another question, Is God limited to 25% compounding? Even though there is no biblical interest rate stated, the Bible does point out in many places that he who sows sparingly shall also reap sparingly, and that God causes fruit to grow at 30-fold, 60-fold, and 100-fold. In percentage terms, 30-fold is 3,000%; 60-fold is 6,000% and 100-fold is 10,000%. I don't believe it is wrong to assume that God's rate of compounding is 3,000%, 6,000%, 10,000%, and even greater.

Then I would ask the question, Is an investment of $10,000, compounding at 25%, comparable to giving the amount of $10,000, compounding at 10,000%, for all eternity? That is the real comparison. Matthew 6:19–24 makes clear that our treasure will either be on earth ($75,231,000) or in heaven ($10,000 x 10,000% x eternity). Without question, the eternal perspective on giving makes the temporal perspective of no consequence.

As someone once said to me, "Do your giving while you're living so you're knowing where it's going." And the martyred missionary, Jim Elliot, said, "He is no fool who gives up what he cannot keep in order to gain what he cannot lose." Whether to give now or later is really a silly question when you put it into the perspective of the Almighty.

God is perfectly able to handle your investment of His resources in His kingdom and to cause it to grow and to compound at the greatest rate. He does not need your expertise nor skill to cause an investment to grow in order to be able to give more later.

Chart 15–B gives you an opportunity to make a faith giving pledge for the coming year. It breaks the faith giving pledge down to the three levels of giving—what you should give, what you could give, and what you would give. You cannot complete this pledge until:

1. You have summarized your financial situation and determined what amount of proportionate giving you are going to do.
2. You know what amount of sacrificial giving you are going to do by giving up something.
3. You know what your cash flow margin is—that which you would give if God caused it to be more than you anticipated.

My challenge for you is to prayerfully make the pledge and then watch what God does to cause it to become a reality!

Chart 15–B

FAITH GIVING PLEDGE

*RECOGNIZING THAT GOD WANTS US TO BE
GOOD STEWARDS OF HIS RESOURCES
AND USE THEM FOR HIS PURPOSES,
WE MAKE THE FOLLOWING
GIVING PLEDGE FOR THE COMING YEAR:*

Amount

What we <u>should</u> give: _____

What we <u>could</u> give by making a sacrifice in the following area:

_____ _____

What we <u>would</u> give if God blesses us with:

_____ _____

We will give: _____

_____
Name

_____
Name

DON'T MISS THE MIRACLE

I have often wondered what it is going to be like to stand before the Lord and have Him evaluate my works. I wonder whether I will hear Him say, "Well done, good and faithful servant; you were faithful over a few things, I will make you ruler over many things. Enter into the joy of your lord" (Matt. 25:21). Or, on the other hand, will I watch as most of the works that I have accomplished are consumed by fire? My greatest fear is that I may fervently work at the wrong task rather than faithfully complete God's work for me.

Mark 6 is a passage on which I often reflect.

The apostles gathered to Jesus and told Him all things, both what they had done and what they had taught. And He said to them, "Come aside by yourselves to a deserted place and rest a while." For there were many coming and going, and they did not even have time to eat. So they departed to a deserted place in the boat by themselves. But the multitudes saw them departing, and many knew Him and ran there on foot from all the cities. They arrived before them and came together to Him. And Jesus, when He came out, saw a great multitude and was moved with compassion for them, because they were like sheep not having a shepherd. So He began to teach them many things. And when the day was now far spent, His disciples came to Him and said, "This is a deserted place, and already the hour is late. Send them away, that they may go into the surrounding country and villages and buy themselves bread; for they have nothing to eat." But He answered and said to them, "You give them something to eat." And they said to Him, "Shall we go and buy two hundred denarii worth of bread and give them something to eat?" But He said to them, "How many loaves do you have? Go and see." And when they found out they said, "Five, and two fish." Then He commanded them to make them all sit down in groups on the green grass. So they sat down in ranks, in hundreds and in fifties. And when He had taken the five loaves and the two fish, He looked up to heaven, blessed and broke the loaves, and gave them to His disciples to set before them; and the two fish He divided among them all. So they all ate and were filled. And they took up twelve baskets full of fragments and of the fish. Now those who had eaten the loaves were about five thousand men (6:30–44).

Many conclusions that are applicable to financial planning can be drawn from this passage because financial planning is, in reality, the working out of the priorities of life. Let's examine the principles I have gleaned from this passage.

Principle 1

Jesus said, "Come aside by yourselves to a deserted place and rest a while" (Mark 6:31). The first step to financial planning is to be alone with Jesus and listen to what He has to say. It is not the development of a plan, it is not getting advice, but it is spending time alone with Him.

Unless you hear God's voice, you cannot take a second step. Jesus recognized this principle, and it is obvious in His life because He spent much time alone with God prior to making any major decision. Can we do less?

Principle 2

"Jesus, when He came out, saw a great multitude and was moved with compassion for them, because they were like sheep not having a shepherd. So He began to teach them many things" (Mark 6:34). A second principle is that our *plan* should not be our god. Jesus had a plan to go with His disciples to a quiet place; however, when He saw the needs, He had compassion on the people and was responsive to God's direction in His life at that point. To be totally committed to a plan is to make a serious mistake. God works in our lives through many circumstances and to ignore them because a plan is in place is to run the risk of missing God's will.

Principle 3

"His disciples came to Him and said, 'This is a deserted place, and already the hour is late. Send them away, that they may go into the surrounding country and villages and buy themselves bread" (Mark 6:35–36). I have often asked myself, What's wrong with this advice? The answer is, nothing—except that it was wrong. It was very practical and logical, but it was not in accordance with what Jesus intended at that point. Two guides come from this passage: First of all, don't ever thwart God because of merely a practical consideration. God wants to do things in His way, in His time. Practicality does not always coincide with faith. It is not wrong in itself; it is just wrong in light of what God wants to accomplish.

The second principle that comes out of this advice is that worldly advice can be logical, but it is not necessarily right. Many Christians fall into the trap of listening to non-Christian counselors and expect the non-Christian counselor to give them godly advice. The advice may sound good and may even be good, but unless it is advice that comes from God, it is wrong.

Principle 4

The disciples argued a bit with Jesus regarding His plan, but Jesus did not argue back. Finally He directed them to have all the people sit down on the grass. This was very illogical because, at that point, they did not have the food to feed them. The principle that comes out of this is that we must be obedient. No questions asked. If God says to do it, I do it. If God says to give, I give. If God says to pay off debt—I do it. If God says to accumulate to pay my taxes, I do so. If God says to increase or decrease my lifestyle, I do so. The issue is *obedience*.

Principle 5

In verse 40, when the disciples had the people sit down on the grass, there were three elements present that are always present in a faith plan. First of all, they obviously could not see how the people were going to be fed. Oftentimes, in a financial plan, we may not see how our goal is going to be accomplished either. Second, there were without question inadequate resources to accomplish the disciples' objective, and that also may be characteristic of our financial plan—that we have inadequate resources. Third, the disciples did not know what the next step was going to be to fulfill God's plan. Thus, a faith plan for us may require action without our full understanding. I think of Noah's building an ark for 100 years, not fully understanding what God was going to do, or Abraham's leaving Ur, not knowing what God was going to do.

Principle 6

Verses 42–43 say, "They all ate and were filled. And they took up twelve baskets full of fragments and of the fish." The results of operating according to a faith plan are that the goal will be reached, God will be glorified, and growth will occur. In the case of the 5,000 the goal was reached, the Lord received the glory, and the disciples *should have* experienced growth in their faith.

However, if you read on in the passage, you come down to verses

51–52, "Then He went up into the boat to them, and the wind ceased. And they were greatly amazed in themselves beyond measure, and marveled. For they had not understood about the loaves, because their heart was hardened." What a tragedy! Just a few hours earlier they had seen an unbelievable miracle. As a matter of fact, they had participated in the miracle by handing out the bread and fish, and then gathering up the twelve baskets. However, the Scripture says, "They were greatly amazed in themselves beyond measure, and marveled. For they had not understood about the loaves, because their heart was hardened."

The challenge is, don't plan God out of your finances. Don't have a closed mind. Don't miss the miracle. I hope that much has been given to you in this book that is practical and useful; but don't miss the miracle of what God wants to do in your life by saying, "It is not appropriate or applicable in my situation, for surely God could not want to do that for me."

God merely wants you to take the first step, then the second step, then the third step, so that when you stand before Him, you will finally understand that whatever has been accomplished has been accomplished by Him. Because of your faithfulness with regard to what He has given you, you will hear Him say, "Well done, good and faithful servant; you were faithful over a few things, I will make you ruler over many things. Enter into the joy of your lord" (Matt. 25:21).

GLOSSARY

AFTER-TAX RETURN—The yield of an investment after taxes have been taken out.

ANNUITY—An individual pays an insurance company a specified capital sum in exchange for a promise that the insurer will, at some time in the future, begin to make a series of periodic payments to the individual for as long as he/she lives or for some other specified period of time.

APPRECIATION—An increase in fair market value.

ASSETS—Everything a person owns, including cash, investments, accounts receivable, real property, autos, and the like.

BALANCE SHEET—A condensed financial statement showing the amount and nature of an individual's assets and liabilities at a given time. A "snapshot" of what a person owns and what he owes. Sometimes referred to as *net worth statement*.

BASIS—The price paid for an asset. Used to figure capital gains tax.

BENEFICIARY—One who is designated to receive a benefit. Example: person who would receive the proceeds of a life insurance settlement.

BID AND ASKED—The "bid" is the highest price anyone is willing to pay for a security at a given time; the "asked" is the lowest price anyone will take at that time. Stocks are usually purchased at "bid" and sold at "asked."

BOND—A promise of a corporation, municipality, government, church, and the like, to pay interest at a stated rate and repay face value of the bond (which is actually a loan from you to the corporation or other entity) at a specified maturity date.

BUDGET—A plan or guideline for spending.

CAPITAL GAIN—Profit or loss from the sale of a capital asset such as real estate, stock, commercial property, land, equipment, and the like. Any capital

229

asset held at least one year is classified as long-term and may receive favorable income tax treatment.

CAPITAL NEEDS—In personal financial planning, the amount of capital (assets or cash) needed in a lump sum to enable one to meet income needs and expenses should death or disability occur.

CASH FLOW—The process of money coming in from various sources (income) and being spent on various uses (expenses). A *cash flow* statement is a look at both the income and the expenses over any period of time, but is usually for at least a month and/or a year.

CASH SURRENDER VALUE—The actual value of your life insurance policy. It is the amount of cash you would receive if you voluntarily terminate your policy before it matures. It is also the amount that can be borrowed from your policy while still keeping the policy in force. This value can be found in the policy contract. It may be more than the contract value as it can be increased by dividends and interest on dividends that are left to accumulate (dividend deposits).

COMMON STOCK—Securities that represent an ownership interest in a corporation. Generally have dividend and appreciation potential.

COST PER THOUSAND—Refers to the cost of each thousand dollars of life insurance protection.

CURRENT ASSETS—Those assets that can easily be converted into cash or sold in a short period of time. Example: stocks, certificates of deposit, cash value of life insurance, money market funds, and the like. Also known as *liquid assets*.

DEBT—A sum owed to someone else, either a financial or personal obligation; a state of owing.

DIVERSIFICATION—Spreading money among different types of investments.

DIVIDEND—The payment designated by a corporation to be distributed pro rata among outstanding shares of stock. Corporations usually declare dividends from their profits, and the amount is in relation to the amount of the profit.

DIVIDEND ELECTION—The method you choose to receive your dividends. Most commonly refers to life insurance. You may elect dividends to be paid in cash, to reduce premiums, to buy paid-up additions, or to accumulate at interest.

DOLLAR COST AVERAGING—A method of purchasing securities at regular intervals with a fixed amount of dollars, regardless of the prevailing prices of the securities. Payments buy more shares when the price is low and fewer shares when it rises. Because of the fluctuations of the market, this method enables an investor who consistently buys in both good and bad times to be able to improve his potential for a gain when he sells. It is an effective method for a single investor to strategically invest his money.

EFFECTIVE RATE—The amount of each dollar earned that goes to pay taxes. The ratio of total taxes paid to gross income.

FACE VALUE—The amount the insurance company promises to pay at death of insured.

FIDUCIARY—One who acts for another in financial matters.

FIXED—Refers to an asset principal that cannot grow in value. You will never get back more or less than you invested. Example: certificates of deposit, cash value, bonds, and the like. These assets are yielding in nature.

INDIVIDUAL RETIREMENT ACCOUNT (IRA)—A retirement provision established by law that allows an individual to deduct from his income a certain amount set aside for future retirement.

INFLATION—An increase in the volume of money and credit relative to available goods resulting in a substantial and continuing rise in the general price level.

INFLATIONARY SPIRAL—A continuous rise in prices which is sustained by the interaction of usage increases and cost increases.

INVESTMENT—The use of money for the purpose of making more money: to gain income, increase capital, save taxes, or a combination of the three.

KEOGH OR SELF-EMPLOYED RETIREMENT PLAN—Similar to an IRA, but designed for the self-employed individual. The Keogh permits the setting aside of a specified part of current earnings for use as a retirement fund in the future.

LEVERAGE—The use of a small amount of equity or assets to control or purchase an asset worth substantially more. The value to the investor is that you receive appreciation on the total worth of the asset, not just your equity. Although leveraging increases your earnings potential, one is "at risk" for the amount leveraged (the loan). Example: If you put $10,000 down and borrow $70,000 to buy an $80,000 home, you have leveraged.

LIABILITIES—All the claims against you. Obligations you owe. Some may be current (owed within the year), such as credit card loans; others may be long-term, such as a home mortgage.

LIQUIDITY—(Liquid) The state of assets readily converted to cash at their current fair market value. (Will not lose value upon sale as a result of a lack of a ready market.)

LONG-TERM ASSETS—(Nonliquid) Those assets that cannot easily be converted to cash or sold or consumed in a short period of time. Example: home, real estate, land assets, and the like.

MARGIN—The cash sources less the cash uses. The amount you have left to spend as you desire after all living expenses, mandatory commitments, and taxes are met.

MARGINAL RATE—The tax bracket percentage from which your income tax is calculated. For example, in the case of a person in the 27% tax bracket, 27¢ of each additional dollar earned would go to the government in taxes.

MARITAL DEDUCTION—In calculating estate tax, a deduction allowed by law against the estate of the first spouse to die. The amount of the qualifying property or deduction under the new Economic Recovery Tax Act of 1981 is the entire estate of the first to die.

MINIMUM DEPOSIT—When the cash value increases in the insurance policy are used to pay the premiums of the policy.

MONEY MARKET FUND—A mutual fund that invests in money market instruments such as Treasury Bills, U. S. Government agency issues, commercial bank certificates of deposit, commercial paper, and the like. The interest rate on a money market fund fluctuates with the prime interest rate.

MORTGAGE—Usually refers to the balance of the loan on a home. The amount of money borrowed to purchase a home.

NONLIQUID—Investments not easily converted to cash at their current fair market value.

PREFERRED STOCK—Similar to common stock. Generally less dividend and appreciation potential but receives a higher *priority* or preference over common stock in dividend payments or in the event of liquidation.

PREMIUM—The payment an insurance policy holder agrees to make for coverage.

PRESENT VALUE—The value of a sum of money to be received in the future in today's dollars taking into account either interest rates, inflation, or both.

PRIME RATE—The interest rate charged by large U. S. money center commercial banks to their best business borrowers.

PRINCIPAL—A person's capital or money. Used for investments. Sometimes referred to as equity when talking about a house.

PROSPECTUS—A circular that describes securities or investments being offered for sale to the public.

PURCHASING POWER—The ability of a dollar to buy a product or service. As prices increase, purchasing power decreases. Today's dollar will not buy as much today as it would in 1970.

UNIFIED CREDIT—A credit, established by law, applied to tentative federal estate taxes owed upon death of an individual.

VARIABLE—Refers to assets that have the potential to grow; primarily concerned with appreciation. Examples: stocks, real estate, and the like. These may be sold for more or less than you invested.

WILL—The directions of a testator (the male or female who makes a will) regarding the final disposition of his or her estate.

WITHHOLDING—Refers to the amount of tax withheld from a paycheck.

WITHHOLDING ALLOWANCES—Used by an employer to calculate the amount withheld monthly from your check for federal and state taxes.

YIELD—Dividends or interest paid by a company expressed as a percentage of current selling price.

Additional Reading

CHRISTIAN

Baldwin, Stanley G. *Your Money Matters*. Minneapolis, Minn.: Bethany, 1977.

Bruso, Dick. *Bible Promises: Help & Hope for Your Finances*. San Bernardino, Calif.: Here's Life, 1985.

Burkett, Larry. *Your Finances in Changing Times*. San Bernardino, Calif.: Campus Crusade for Christ, 1975.

Clouse, Robert G. *Wealth and Poverty*. Downers Grove, Ill.: InterVarsity Press, 1984.

Davis, John Jefferson. *Your Wealth in God's World*. Phillipsburg, N.J.: Presbyterian and Reformed, 1984.

Dayton, Edward R., and Ted W. Engstrom. *Strategy for Living*. Glendale, Calif.: Gospel Light, 1976.

Dayton, Howard L., Jr. *Your Money: Frustration or Freedom?* Wheaton, Ill.: Tyndale, 1979.

Flynn, Leslie B. *Your God and Your Gold*. Williamsport, Pa.: Hearthstone, 1973.

Fooshee, Jr., George. *You Can Be Financially Free*. Old Tappan, N.J.: Revell, 1976.

Fooshee, George and Marjean Fooshee. *You Can Beat the Money Squeeze*. Old Tappan, N.J.: Revell, 1980.

Fries, Michael and C. Holland Taylor. *A Christian Guide to Prosperity*. Oakland, Calif.: Communication Research, 1984.

Hutka, Ed. *$ Boom or Busted*. Plainfield, N.J.: Logos International, 1980.

MacArthur, John, Jr. *God's Plan for Giving*. Panorama City, Calif.: Word of Grace Communications, 1979.

Murray, Andrew. *Christ's Perspective on the Use and Abuse of Money*. Minneapolis, Minn.: Bethany, 1978.

235

Olford, Stephen. *The Grace of Giving: Thoughts on Financial Stewardship*. Grand Rapids, Mich.: Zondervan, 1972.

Tam, Stanley. *God Owns My Business*. Alberta, Canada: Horizon House, 1969.

Watts, John G. *Leave Your House In Order: A Guide To Planning Your Estate*. Wheaton, Ill.: Tyndale, 1979.

Webley, Simon. *How to Give Away Your Money*. Downers Grove, Ill.: InterVarsity Press, 1978.

SECULAR
Caspel, Venita Van. *Money Dynamics for the 80's*. Reston, Va.: Reston Publishing Company, 1980.

Clason, George S. *The Richest Man in Babylon*. New York: Hawthorn Books, 1955.

Kinzel, Robert K. *Retirement*. New York: AMACOM, 1979.

Stillman, Richard J. *Guide to Personal Finance: A Lifetime Program of Money Management*. Englewood Cliffs, N.J.: Prentice-Hall, 1979.